RAISE
the SONG

RAISE *the* SONG

A Classical Christian
Guide to Music Education

EDITED BY
JARROD RICHEY

ACCS
PUBLICATIONS

RAISE THE SONG: A Classical Christian Guide to Music Education

Copyright © 2019 ACCS Publications
Association of Classical Christian Schools

All rights reserved. No part of this publication may be reproduced, distributed, or transmitted in any form or by any means, including photocopying, recording, or other electronic or mechanical methods, without the prior written permission of the publisher, except in the case of brief quotations embodied in critical reviews and certain other noncommercial uses permitted by copyright law.

ISBN: 978-0-578-52016-2 (Paperback)

Cover design: Rachel Rosales
Interior design: Jarrod Richey

First printing edition 2019.

Association of Classical Christian Schools
P.O. Box 9741
317 W 6th St., STE 211
Moscow, ID 83843

www.classicalchristian.org
www.accsedu.org

CONTENTS

PREFACE | *David Goodwin* — 7

INTRODUCTION | *Jarrod Richey* — 13

SECTION ONE: PHILOSOPHY

1. The Sounds of Wisdom and Virtue — 19
   Dr. Steve Turley

2. Classical vs. Progressive Education — 41
   David Goodwin

3. Take Everything Captive to Christ — 49
   Kent Young

SECTION TWO: PRACTICE

4. The Singing School — 67
   Jarrod Richey

5. Joyful Music Literacy — 83
   Jarrod Richey

6. Wisdom in Music Program Building — 107
   Dr. David Erb

7. Resource Recommendations — 125
   Dr. David Erb & Jarrod Richey

APPENDIX | To the Administrator — 139
David Goodwin

PREFACE

DAVID GOODWIN

When you live in the bland shallows of our culture, and you first encounter something true, good, and beautiful, it will seem confrontational—at least for an instant. Like the blades of grass in Lewis' *The Great Divorce*, the discomfort of the real or transcendent drives many away from a wonderful place. Visitors enter our schools and see uniforms, order, articulate children, and beauty. Their senses confront them. This should be the case. Not because they have encountered something offensive. But, rather, because their senses have been tuned by our culture to a dissonant chord, played by an increasingly Christless world. The song we are playing stands in stark contrast to that.

As the President of the Association of Classical Christian Schools, I've traveled and visited many schools. The music programs in those schools tell a story. On one trip, I was invited to join the grammar schoolers as they sang a catchy but kitschy camp song popular for children in evangelical church circles. On the same trip, at a different school, I listened to a group of late-grammar school students sing a great hymn, complete with beautiful harmonies. Then again, I've heard great hymns, sung poorly, or tunes that were not beautiful at other schools. The contrast between these experiences saddened me. We have nearly 16,000 hours with the kids, true. Yet that's so little time. We should not squander any of it. ACCS schools started over two decades ago with a commitment to take every aspect of our lives captive in obedience to Christ. This requires a constant retuning of every aspect of our schools so the three-part harmony of truth, goodness, and beauty resonates in our halls, all of them.

Welcome to the ACCS Distinctive School Series. We've commissioned this series of books for this purpose: We want your school to reflect a harmony that lifts the hearts of visitors, students, and parents alike because they encounter a real difference between your school and their expectations. And we want this harmony to penetrate beyond the surface into the deepest foundations of your school. It is better to be than to seem. Therefore, we've released a series of "Distinctive School" articles within the ACCS Member Resource Center online tool covering a number of areas of importance. But, some tuning needs to go deeper than articles can do. These books support the central tuning pegs on which our schools rest. They are intended to define the outlines of classical Christian education for schools. Think of the series as survey stakes put on a building site to outline the future building. Classical education is too big to contain in one series. We wouldn't be so bold. We're choosing those topics that we believe must first define the outlines of every classical school. We expect there to be about a dozen stakes in the ground by the time the series is finished. We'll see what the Lord does with it.

Throughout this series, the ACCS will draw upon the thought-leaders that have emerged over the years in our movement. They've created some of the best programs available within our schools.

PREFACE

DR. DAVID R. ERB is a Fellow of Music at New Saint Andrews College in Moscow, ID. He received his Doctor of Musical Arts in conducting from the University of Wisconsin-Madison. He has taught in multiple ACCS schools and served as a Chief Musician in multiple CREC Churches. He is the composer of *Cantica Sanctorum*, a collection of 50 through-composed psalm settings and other sacred music for congregations.

DR. STEVE TURLEY (PhD, Durham University) is an internationally recognized scholar, speaker, and classical guitarist. He is the author of over 20 books, including *Classical vs. Modern Education: A Vision from C.S. Lewis* and *Awakening Wonder: A Classical Guide to Truth, Goodness, and Beauty*. Steve's popular YouTube channel showcases weekly his expertise in the rise of nationalism, populism, and traditionalism throughout the world, and his podcasts and writings on civilization, society, culture, education, and the arts are widely accessed at TurleyTalks.com. He is a faculty member at Tall Oaks Classical School in Bear, DE, where he teaches Theology and Rhetoric, and was previously a Professor of Fine Arts at Eastern University.

JARROD RICHEY is the Music Program Director and Director of Choral Activities at Geneva Academy in West Monroe, Louisiana where he has been teaching general music and choir since 2008. He holds a Masters of Music Degree from the University of Louisiana Monroe. Additionally, he received his Kodály music teacher certification from Wichita State University. He has presented numerous sessions and workshops for the ACCS on music in recent years. He is the author of *Bach to the Future: Fostering Music Literacy Today*. He is serving as the general editor of this book.

KENT YOUNG is a music teacher at The Oaks Classical Christian Academy in Spokane Valley, Washington, where he has taught general music, choir, and New Testament since 2006. He received a Masters of Music Degree from Colorado State University where he studied choral conducting and vocal performance. He has taught and directed music programs for 19 years in Christian schools and churches in Colorado and Washington.

It may seem surprising that we didn't start with "the trivium" or "science," but our goal is the cultivation of rightly ordered affections to help shape virtuous and wise Christians. If we earnestly pursue this goal, then we must begin with those things that shape our communities. After all, we need Christian communities that are distinct and beautiful for a day such as this. In Francis Schaeffer's *Trilogy*, he recounts the twentieth century's walk away from Christ and toward the ugliness of atheistic secularism. In *Trilogy*, he points to the ugliness of modern graphic art and its reflection of the ugliness of the post-Christian worldview. Music could not follow graphic art all the way into despair. Despite attempts of musicians to slam on piano keys randomly, it was too offensive. This should tell us something. As Saul sought David's harp to soothe his tortured soul, as God filled the book of Psalms to be His longest tribute in scripture, as the medievals cast their cosmology in the music of the spheres, and as C.S. Lewis depicts Aslan singing

PREFACE

into creation all that exists, we should notice something. Music is powerful. With great power comes the need for great care. And despite the fact that I really am not a musician myself, I sought out music to be the first in this series because of that power. As you read this, I hope you will see why.

INTRODUCTION

JARROD RICHEY

Where there is no vision, the people perish: but he that keepeth the law, happy is he. –Proverbs 29:18

The Scriptures remind us that vision is essential for a people to flourish. For music education to thrive within our classical Christian school community, the vision must be clear and attainable. The goal of this book is to present a philosophical case as well as a practical model for music education within the classical Christian school paradigm.

The pursuit of Truth, Goodness, and Beauty is a common slogan of classical Christian schools. Truth and Goodness have been cultivated with great diligence, but Beauty is still waiting its turn. Ask any student trained in a classical Christian school, "What is the standard for truth?" and they will answer, "God." "And Goodness?" "God defines what is Good too." But ask that same student, "What is the standard for beauty?" Though the answer is the same, students are not so quick to declare it. It is no wonder, because they are situated in a culture that believes beauty is relative. The visual and performing arts have paid profoundly for this perspective. Music in particular, once recognized as a core mathematical discipline within the quadrivium, is now considered extracurricular, its loveliness defined by the preferences of the listener instead of the triune God.

In this work, you will hear from those who have been working in the field of music within the ACCS community. The authors seek to answer the "why?" of music education as well as lay out a vision for the "how?" From the outset, you will be challenged to view your thinking about music in terms of a broader, historical context. The authors also provide a practical sketch of how to bring these ideas to fruition.

This book is not intended to present a finalized curriculum. Ask anyone to think back on their favorite class in school, and they will remember the name of that teacher better than the textbook or curriculum. The music teacher demonstrates this truth in particular. The authors recognize this and emphasize the importance of the music teacher's qualifications (both in skill and heart) over the particular curriculum used. There are no gimmicks or formulas that place music training on the fast track, and the classical Christian model of education should resist the temptation to believe such ploys. Whether a school board member, head of school, music teacher, or parent, the reader of this book should keep this theme in mind. As Douglas Wilson has encouraged educators and churchgoers over the years, agreement on the principles is paramount, but there is room for variance in the methods used to apply those principles.

Within the area of music education, there are many methods available for training students. Keeping a right goal in mind will help filter out the unhelpful ones. Simply stated, the goal of music education is the joyful music literacy of *all* students. They should be trained to read, write, sing, and make music as they are trained in their native language. There are flashy substitutes to this that can be paraded out in front of our schools, but these only give an illusion of music literacy. Far too many students have taken music in the form of choir, band, or private lessons and continued on in life unequipped for enjoyment and growth in music.

By the end of this book, I hope you will be able to echo the sentiment of the cabbie in C.S. Lewis' *The Magician's Nephew*, who, upon hearing Aslan's glorious singing at the creation of Narnia, exclaimed quite aptly, "Glory be! I'd ha' been a better man all my life if I'd known there were things like this." Regardless of the role you play in your school's mission, we hope this collaborative work informs, retunes, encourages, and equips you with renewed vision and vitality towards a robust recovery of music literacy in classical Christian schools for His glory.

SECTION ONE

PHILOSOPHY

1

The SOUNDS of WISDOM and VIRTUE

How to Think about Music as a Classical Christian Educator

STEPHEN R. TURLEY, PH.D

INTRODUCTION

The last notes of the Sanctus from the early seventeenth-century English composer William Byrd's *Mass for Four Voices* faded into silence. Turning off the CD player, I sat down in front of about twenty college students. For many, this was their first attentive hearing of renaissance polyphony. "So, what do you think?" I asked them. A hand raised from the back of the classroom, followed by the rather disappointing response: "I found it kinda boring." My classical sensibilities kicked in: "Ok, but should you have?" "What do you mean?" my student asked incredulously and somewhat defensively, "It's just my opinion." "I understand," I reassured her, "but is your opinion correct?" Her brows furled and she said, "It's music. There is no correct answer. It's *all* a matter of opinion."

The musical perspective that dominates our age is what we might call aesthetic *relativism*. The relativist view sees music as entirely personal and intuitive; there is no objective basis for determining whether one kind or form of music is 'better' than another. Music is simply a matter of subjective taste and personal preference, and bears no resemblance at all to the categories that lend themselves to objective evaluation, such as mathematics and the sciences.

This view is profoundly flawed. It is inextricably linked to a consumerist mentality that reduces music to a mere commodity, which is appropriated as a prepackaged formulaic that serves mass utility goals through global distribution channels. The life expectancy of a song in this cultural context is brief, the average radio lifespan being no more than a few months. Indeed, a study was released recently that suggested playing a chart hit for more than four months may affect adversely the ratings of a radio station.[1] This sonic commodification stands in stark contrast to the music of many other cultures outside the West, some of which celebrate tunes and melodies that have lasted for more than a thousand years.

Unfortunately, despite its rich musical tradition, this relativism has not passed over the church. A particularly striking example comes from Rick Warren. In his 1995 mega-hit, *The Purpose Driven Church*, he writes:

> I reject the idea that music styles can be judged as either 'good' or 'bad' music. Who decides this? The kind of music you like is determined by your

---

1. "Overplaying Songs is Dangerous Business," *Radio Analyzer*, accessed April 4, 2019, http://www.radioanalyzer.com/overplaying_songs_is_dangerous_business.pdf.

background and culture ... Churches also need to admit that no particular *style* of music is 'sacred.' What makes a song sacred is its *message*. Music is nothing more than an arrangement of notes and rhythms; it's the words that make a song spiritual.[2]

According to a 2005 Barna survey of American pastors, *The Purpose Driven Church* was cited as the second most influential book in their lives.[3]

One need look no further than our institutions of Christian education to see how pervasive this relativistic view of music has become. I have found that students at both the Christian school and university where I taught, when called to give a basic account for the classical conception of art and beauty, have given answers to my inquiries which consistently exemplify a complete and total devotion to aesthetic relativism. I am not exaggerating in the least. As classical educators, administrators, and parents, we often find ourselves at a loss for communicating such a vision of music to our students. In an age of iPods and iPads, commodification and consumerism has redefined not only the world of music, but the world as expressed and interpreted by music. It is virtually unthinkable among us to hear our Top 40 hits as echoes of a cosmos resonating with divine harmonies, and attempts at teaching such on the part of the educator appear artificially forced if not unintelligible.

---

2. Rick Warren, *The Purpose Driven Church: Growth without Compromising Your Message and Mission* (Grand Rapids: Zondervan, 1995), 281.

3. "Survey Reveals The Books and Authors That Have Most Influenced Pastors," Barna Group, May 30, 2005, accessed April 4, 2019, https://www.barna.com/research/survey-reveals-the-books-and-authors-that-have-most-influenced-pastors/.

However, as with the example of the student above, I have found that we can in fact resolve such obstacles; there is a rich tapestry of concepts, vocabulary, and listening examples that we can tap into to teach and awaken students to a classical vision of music. But first, we as teachers, administrators, and parents have to overcome our own obstacles that impede us from experiencing music in its fullest classical expression.[4] This chapter will explore precisely what this classical conception of music entails, how the classical conception contrasts with the aesthetics of contemporary pop music, and how the educator can teach students to love music in a distinctively classical manner that makes room for both classical and contemporary music.

MUSIC AND THE DIVINE ORDER OF THE COSMOS

The representation of music in the Old Testament is inextricably bound up with the whole created order. The Septuagint, the ancient Greek translation of the Hebrew Scriptures, explicitly links creation with Beauty. In the original Hebraic version of the Genesis creation account, a responsive refrain accompanies each one of God's creative actions: 'and it was good.' The word there for 'good' is the Hebrew, *tov*. However, when it was translated into the Greek in the third century

---

4. By 'classical,' I'm not referring solely to the music genre by that name, much less to the term used by musicologists and historians to specify that musical period between the mid-eighteenth to early-nineteenth centuries. Instead, I mean the conception and practice of music that echoed a universe full of divine meaning and purpose, a cosmos that resonated with stunning correspondences and grand harmonies that became audible in music making and composition. For a more in-depth development of a classical conception of music, see my book, *Echoes of Eternity: A Classical Guide to Music* (Camp Hill: Classical Academic Press, 2018).

before Christ, the translators rendered the term for 'good' as *kallos*, which not only means 'beautiful,' but is related etymologically to *kalein*, 'to call.'

It is this interpretation of Genesis that overlapped with other passages of Scripture to inspire both Jewish and Christian traditions to see God as creating the world as a grand symphony. The Book of Job describes how the morning stars sang together and the sons of God shouted for joy as the world was created.[5] In the Septuagint version of Proverbs, Wisdom was with God holding all things together in harmony.[6] This vision of the world created through heavenly song captured the imagination of C.S. Lewis when he wrote *The Magician's Nephew*, where Aslan sings the world of Narnia into being, creating Narnia through song.

Throughout the Old Testament, the creation itself is depicted as a great Temple: God sets the foundations, He stretches the heavens as a canopy, and we are here to pick up on that song of creation and make it manifest, make it audible in the world (cf. Psalm 104). The 'new song' (cf. Psalms 93, 96, 98) that resounded in the House of the Lord echoed the heavenly song that awakened the world into being, and thus perpetuated the life of creation.

Music for the Jewish imagination thus revealed the world to be an arena of divine creation. Indeed, it could be viewed that music was itself a manifestation of the presence of God. Upon the return of the Ark of the Covenant to the tabernacle, the Chronicler describes how David appointed musicians "to invoke, to thank and to praise the Lord the God of Israel" (1 Chron. 16:4). Once Solomon's temple was finished,

---

5. Job 38:7.

6. Margaret Barker, "Temple Music," http://tandtclark.typepad.com/ttc/2009/06/margaret-barker-on-temple-music.html (blog), June 4, 2009, accessed April 4, 2019.

the Levitical choir praised and thanked the Lord "with one voice," and then the glory of the Lord filled the temple.⁷ The connection between music and the presence of God may be found in the Hebrew term for 'praise,' *hll*, which also means 'shine.' The music of the Levitical choir thus invoked the radiance of the presence of God.

The Hebrews were not alone in conceiving of the cosmos as an arena of divine song. The Ionian Greek philosopher Pythagoras (ca. 570-490 BC) imagined that the entire cosmos is subject to the same laws of proportion that rule music, such that all things form a great harmony. This term, *harmonia*, for the Greeks, is not so much a musical term as it is a cosmic one. Harmony is first and foremost a cosmic mathematical principle which involves a blending and combining of opposites into a grand system, a cosmic structure where all things are related to each other. Pythagoras links together the mathematics that comprise the basis for music with the idea that there are underlying mathematical harmonies throughout the entire cosmos to come up with his concept of the 'music of the spheres.' Pythagoras envisions the harmoniousness of the whole universe, such that each of these planets and star systems has its own different tonal sequence. And thus it is the combination of the stars and the planets that makes the sounds of the heavenly spheres.

The important point here is that music for the Greeks and the wider classical tradition was not so much understood as something performed, composed, practiced, or played; rather music was interpreted as a mathematical discipline, which sought to discover and formalize the symmetrical relations between sounds.⁸ It was an integral component

---

7. 2 Chronicles 5:11-14.

8. Carol Harrison, "Augustine and the Art of Music," in *Resonant Witness: Conversations between Music and Theology.* eds. Jeremy S. Begbie, Steve R. Guthrie (Grand Rapids: Eerdmans, 2011), 27-45, 27.

to the mathematical disciplines that comprised the *quadrivium*: arithmetic, geometry, music, and astronomy. For the classical mind, arithmetic revealed 'number in itself,' geometry revealed 'number in space,' music revealed 'number in time,' and astronomy revealed 'number in space and time.' In this sense, music was an integral part of the Greek educational curriculum which functioned as a metaphor for this whole cosmic chain of interrelationships and harmonies. Indeed, Plato could say: "The whole choral art is also in our view the whole of education" (*Laws* Bk II). The Greeks understood the nature of reality and its systems of relations in musical terms.

Christians transfigured this cosmic vision of music found among the Jews and Greeks by re-envisioning it as incorporated into the transformative life, death, and resurrection of Christ. For it is in Christ that both the Temple-filling glory of God on the one hand and the music of the spheres on the other converge. Note how both traditions appear evident on the night of Christ's birth, when the angelic host sang of the reunification of heaven and earth in Christ: "Glory to God in the highest, and on earth peace, good will toward men".[9] Similarly, in his heavenly vision, John describes how "every creation which is in heaven and on the earth, and under the earth, and such as are in the sea," praised God saying: "Blessings, and honour, and glory, and power, be unto him that sitteth upon the throne, and unto the Lamb for ever and ever".[10] In reuniting heaven and earth in his own divinity and humanity, Christ awakens the sounds of heavenly glory in and through the resonance of the spheres.

Christian apologists such as Clement of Alexandria (c.150-c.215) reshaped the Pythagorean concept of the music of the spheres by

---

9. Luke 2:14.

10. Revelation 5:13.

presenting Christ as "the minstrel who imparts harmony to the universe and makes music to God."[11] Clement's successor Origen envisioned a cosmic chorus in Christian worship:

> For we sing hymns to the one God who is over all and his only begotten Word, who is God also. So we sing to God and his only begotten as do the sun, the moon, the stars and the entire heavenly host. For all these form a sacred chorus and sing hymns to the God of all and his only begotten along with those among men who are just.[12]

Augustine (354-430) developed this even further in his *De Musica* with the conception that the numbers of music derive from the unchanging order of eternal numbers which themselves proceed from God. Indeed, Augustine concludes his study in Book VI with the insight that God *is* music. In other words, God *is* perfect symmetry, proportionality, unity, diversity, harmony, and number.[13] For Augustine, when God formed the world from nothing, the *form* was itself music. Thus the entire chain of created being is held together and sustained by music.

And it all came together with the music theory of Boethius (480-524 AD) in the early sixth-century. In his *Principles of Music,* he structured music according to the three-fold pattern of the music of the spheres, the music of the natural world, and the music of the soul. His treatise, which was transmitted throughout the Latin West, was

---

11. Avery Cardinal Dulles, *A History of Apologetics* (Eugene: Wipf and Stock Publishers, 1997), 39-40.

12. Origen, "Against Celsus VIII," 67, quoted in James McKinnon, *Music in Early Christian Literature* (Cambridge: Cambridge University Press, 1987), 38.

13. Harrison, "Augustine," 31.

inordinately influential for the next thousand years. Indeed, Boethius' *Principles of Music* was the music theory textbook used at Oxford until as recently as 1856.[14]

In the Christian synthesis of the Jewish and Greek traditions, music revealed the presence of God on earth through the mediation of the heavens, that is, through the numbers, symmetries, consonances, and unities of the cosmos. While we cannot hear this cosmic music (in that we are too far and fallen), we do have access to the mathematics and principles of symmetry by which that music constantly sounds. This is reflected in the Greek word, *symmetria*, which means 'beautiful.' By awakening the music of the heavens on earth through the study of mathematical proportionality and symmetry, we are able to embody such cosmic harmony and thus transform into heavenly beings.

MUSIC AND THE SANCTIFICATION OF THE SOUL

This *transformative* significance of music is key. Music was considered a divinely ordained instrument for the sanctification of the soul.[15] Plato's pursuit of the Good in his *Republic* outlines his *musikē paideia*, how music and poetry provide the chief means by which rhythm and harmony could be communicated through the body and sunk deeply into the recesses of the soul.[16] And because the Beauty of music communicates Truth and Goodness to the whole soul, bringing harmony to our rational, volitional, and aesthetic capacities, the music

---

14. Robert Reilly, "The Music of the Spheres" *The Imaginative Conservative*, May 24, 2014, accessed April 4, 2019, https://theimaginativeconservative.org/2012/02/music-of-spheres.html.

15. Donald Jay Grout and Claude V. Palisca, *A History of Western Music* (New York: Norton, 2001), 6. This is often referred to as the "doctrine of ethos" in Hellenistic musical thought and practice.

16. Andrew Louth, *The Origins of the Christian Mystical Tradition: From Plato to Denys* (Oxford: Oxford University Press, 1981), 8.

of the cosmos always involves the awakening of *arête*, the classical virtues (wisdom, moderation, justice, and courage) which results when the intellectual, moral, and emotional constituents of our souls reflect the balance or harmony of the cosmos (cf. *Republic* 442A).[17]

As we noted with Boethius' conception of the music of the soul, it is within this cosmic and intellectual milieu that the early church developed a profound sense of the *formative* significance of music for the human person. Athanasius' extended discussion of the psalms observes that singing was ordained to benefit the soul, "because as harmony creates a single concord in joining together the two pipes of the aulos, so … reason will that a man be not disharmonious with himself, nor at variance with himself …" (*Epistula ad Marcellinum de interpretation psalmorum* 27).[18] The facilitation of this inner harmony is a necessary constituent of music: "Just as we make known and signify the thoughts of the soul through the words we express, so too the Lord wished the melody of the words to be a sign of the spiritual harmony of the soul, and ordained that the canticles be sung with melody and the psalms read with song" (*Epistula ad Marcellinum* 28).[19]

Basil of Caesarea understood the Psalms as a chief means of shaping a wise and harmonious soul: "Thus he [the Holy Spirit] contrived for us these harmonious psalm tunes, so that those who are children in actual age as well as those who are young in behavior, while appearing only to sing would in reality be

---

17. Basil Cole, *Music and Morals: A Theological Appraisal of the Moral and Psychological Effects of Music* (Staten Island, NY: Abba House, 1993), 15-45. For a helpful overview of the classical conception of harmonia and its relationship to virtue.

18. McKinnon, *Music in Early*, 53.

19. Ibid., 53.

training their souls" (*Homilia in psalm i*).[20] In the same sermon, Basil spoke of a psalm as "tranquility of soul and the arbitration of peace; it settles one's tumultuous and seething thoughts. It mollifies the soul's wrath and chastens its recalcitrance."[21]

Basil is foregrounding what really is the essence of the classical conception of music: music in many respects was a *mediator* between the divine order of the cosmos and the human soul, which sonically served to cultivate wisdom and virtue within the listener. Augustine described this interrelationship between the moral order of the cosmos with the human person in terms of what he called *ordo amoris*, or the right ordering of our loves. For Augustine, the entire cosmos is comprised of hierarchically ordered goods. At the top, we have the *summum bonum*, the supreme good, which is God himself, who is Goodness in its most immutable and eternal existence, that Good of which none greater can be conceived. However, in light of his doctrine of creation, Augustine sees this Good as constituting a measure or standard in relation to which all finite and temporal constituents derive their goodness.

For Augustine, all things are good in relation to their divinely designated position within the hierarchy of God's creation. Things are not evil in and of themselves but become evil when their order is abused. For example, a ham sandwich is good in itself, but if someone prioritizes the ham sandwich above say a child, then God's hierarchy of goods has been violated. All things are to be valued and loved in accordance with their proportionate value in the divine economy. Augustine develops this notion of virtue as ordered loves (*ordo amoris*) in his *On Christian Doctrine*. In Book I, chapters 3-4, he makes a distinction between things that are enjoyed and things that are used. We enjoy things when we love them for their own sakes; we use things when we love them for the sake of something else. For Augustine, only

---

20. Ibid., 65.
21. Ibid., 65.

God is worthy of being loved for his own sake, for he alone is supremely valuable. All other loves are subordinate to the love of God; all created things are to be loved as objects that cause us to delight in God.

Augustine's conception of *ordo amoris* explains well the ancient notion of music: through the sonic revelation of the mathematical patterns of perfection upon which the entire cosmos is modeled, music revealed to the human soul the divine order of the cosmos and invited the soul, through Beauty, to order its loves and desires in accordance with that divine order. Music both cultivated wisdom (by revealing the cosmic order of goods) and virtue (by aligning our loves with that cosmic order) in the listener. We can thus see that music was considered profoundly *moral*: the job of the composer was to reveal the world as recreated in Christ and thereby facilitate the sanctification of the soul in the cultivation of wisdom and virtue. To the extent that our musical tastes and sensibilities are in the service of this larger cosmic reality, they are consonant with this redemptive vision.

THE CONTEMPORARY CONCEPTION OF MUSIC

The contemporary conception of music, more popularly known as rock'n'roll,[22] ironically stems from the same ecclesiastical soil as the classical vision of music. Many people do not realize that rock music actually came out of the Southern Pentecostal church in the early 1950s. The church served as the space for blending together the three main musical genres that syncretized into rock'n'roll: African rhythm (placing a primacy on drums), rhythm and blues instrumentation (namely the guitar), and gospel melodies and progressions. The first

---

22. Steve Turner, *Hungry for Heaven: Rock 'n' Roll & the Search for Redemption* (Downers Grove, IL: InterVarsity Press, 1995). I, like Steve Turner, use the terms "rock'n'roll" and "rock music" and "pop music" interchangeably and generically to denote everything from rap to rockabilly.

rock'n'roll stars all came out of this Southern Pentecostal space: Elvis Presley, Jerry Lee Lewis (the cousin of Jimmy Swaggart), and Little Richard. In fact his song, "Tutti Frutti" and its iconic refrain *"Awopbopaloobop alopbamboom,"* is a parody of sorts on the Pentecostal practice of speaking in tongues.[23]

As rock'n'roll became an effective medium for radically personal expressions of redemption, it also significantly deviated from the classical conception of music. While classical aesthetics emphasize the objective forms of musical compositions (such as the mathematically derived symmetries and consonances), rock aesthetics are centered more on the subjectivity of the listener.[24] The classical conception of music sees musical form as reflective of the mathematical properties which serve as mediators between heaven and earth; thus the emphasis in classical music is the conforming of our sensibilities, dispositions, and inclinations towards the patterns of perfection entailed in the music. By contrast, rock music is far more concerned on the immediate effect on the listener, and as such, tends to overturn the objectivity of classical aesthetics.[25] While classical music focuses on *objective form*, rock music emphasizes *subjective effect*.

For example, a key characteristic of rock music is its rhythm. Rooted in the southern Pentecostal synthesis of African beat, one of the original intended effects of rock music was the stimulation of the body

---

23. Ibid., 21.

24. Bruce Baugh, "Prolegomena to Any Aesthetics of Rock Music," *The Journal of Aesthetics and Art Criticism*, Vol. 51, No. 1 (Winter, 1993): 23-29, 23.

25. Ibid., 27. Baugh gives the example of Joe Cocker's rendition of "With a Little Help from My Friends," which in many respects is a radical deviation from the Beatles' original recording, and yet it was well received. Had a classical musician taken such liberties with, say, Bach's Chaconne, he would find that critics and audiences are not nearly so tolerant, since it is the score itself that sets the limitations.

for dancing. Hence, the body is of central importance in rock music; if it moves the body, then the song is aesthetically good; if it does not move the body, the song is aesthetically bad. Again, this stands in stark contrast to the classical conception of music, the goodness of which is found in its form which in turn invites the soul and body to conform to it. Note the movement of the human body in ballet, where the body becomes in a sense pure form through the illusion of effortless weightlessness among the dancers.[26] In ballet, the body actually seeks to transcend itself and become united with heavenly form; conversely, in rock music, the body is radically affirmed, and finds its own forms for rhythmic expression, such as head-banging, foot-stomping, or hip-gyrating.

However, it is precisely in this distinctive conformity to the body that rock'n'roll reveals its major difference with the classical conception of music, for while rock's emphasis on the subjective body renders it a powerful form of worship (both originally and in its contemporary Christian resurgence), such subjectivity also renders it vulnerable to moral relativism. The contemporary conception of music is thus inherently *morally ambiguous*, which frustrates and indeed significantly limits its capacity to shape and form the listener's loves and desires to conform to the objective order of God's economy of goods. Indeed, contemporary music is neither equipped nor interested in conforming the loves of the listener to a redemptive vision of the cosmic order, but rather seeks, in consumerist fashion, to conform itself to the desires and loves that already exist within the listener. This moral ambiguity has to be understood if the classical educator is going to appreciate powerful subjectivity of contemporary pop music while maintaining the moral objectivity necessary for the cultivation of wisdom and virtue.

---

26. Baugh, "Prolegomena," 26.

SYNTHESIZING THE CLASSICAL AND CONTEMPORARY CONCEPTIONS OF MUSIC

I do not think that the moral ambiguity of contemporary rock music ought to encourage the educator to renounce or repudiate pop music entirely; such aesthetic dismissals do little good in cultivating the musical tastes and sensibilities of our students. Instead, the *ordo amoris* provides us with a wonderful opportunity to rightly appropriate pop music within the divine economy of goods. Think about a wedding; traditional music, indeed the classical conception of music, fits perfectly with the wedding ceremony proper, while pop music is of course most appropriate for the festivities of the reception. One could easily imagine the incoherence resulting from switching the music. The solemnity or levity of the music reflects the proportionate sensibilities of the occasion. Thus, in affairs of celebration as in the wedding ceremony or on adrenaline-infused occasions such as sports competition, a comparably celebratory or instinctive music from the spectrum of contemporary offerings is only fitting.

However, when it comes to occasions that require a sense of reverence and awe, contemplation and cogitation, the classical conception of music provides the very mediation that evokes such dispositions. Note what theologian David Bentley Hart has observed about the music of Bach:

> Bach is the greatest of Christian theologians, the most inspired witness to the *ordo amoris* in the fabric of being; not only is no other composer capable of more freely developing lines or of more elaborate structures of tonal mediation ... but no one as compellingly demonstrates that the infinite is beauty and that beauty is infinite. It is in Bach's music, as nowhere else, that the potential boundlessness of thematic development becomes manifest: how

a theme can unfold inexorably through difference, while remaining continuous in each moment of repetition, upon a potentially infinite surface of varied repetition ... Bach's is the ultimate Christian music; it reflects as no other human artifact ever has or could the Christian vision of creation.[27]

In encountering the music of Bach, we encounter a music that never has to end; its mathematical intricacies are as seemingly endless as mathematics itself. Hence, it is through Bach's music that we sonically encounter eternity, discovering and rediscovering anew the limitless aesthetic pleasures that such music directs and shapes within our souls. This is quite different from the music of Justin Bieber; while Bach reflects the divine order of creation, Bieber's music reflects the fleeting fads of consumption. This is not to say that Bieber's music is bad; quite the contrary, it is certainly good to the extent that it fulfills a rock'n'roll aesthetic of the body. It *is* to say that if our sensibilities are limited *only* to contemporary music akin to Bieber, then we have largely lost music's formative dimension over our lives.

Bach, like all composers in the classical tradition, is able to awaken such formative sensibilities through what appear to be an unlimited array of musical *gestures*. In order to underscore this point, I like to introduce students to Antonio Vivaldi's violin concerto entitled *La primavera*, or *Spring*. Vivaldi's concerto is based on[28] an Italian sonnet that reads:

---

27. David Bentley Hart, *The Beauty of the Infinite: The Aesthetics of Christian Truth* (Grand Rapids: Eerdmans, 2003), 282-3.

28. Paul Everett, *Vivaldi: The Four Seasons and Other Concertos, Op. 8* (Cambridge: Cambridge University Press, 1996), 76. Given that we don't know the author of the sonnet or the date of its composition, there is controversy as to whether the writing of the sonnet precedes Vivaldi's composition or whether it was written afterwards. Some have

Joyful spring has arrived,
the birds greet it with their cheerful song,
and the brooks in the gentle breezes
flow with a sweet murmur.

The sky is covered with a black mantle,
and thunder and lightning announce a storm.
When they fall silent, the little birds
take up again their melodious song.

Vivaldi uses a combination of the three elements of music —melody, harmony, rhythm—to create musical gestures that mimic the content of the sonnet. For example, we can hear about thirty seconds in, a solo violin enters, with high pitched trills that mimic the singing of birds. Other violins join in to create the effect of numerous birds chirping and tweeting throughout the countryside. The springtide of bird song is then wrapped up with the answering theme at the beginning played by the whole string orchestra, thereby creating a sense of form and return. Then, shortly thereafter, we hear the rushing in of storm winds as per the text of the sonnet above ("The sky is covered with a black mantle, and thunder and lightning announce a storm"). You'll notice how the effect is achieved through a combination of tremolo, an increase in the rapidity of notes, as well as a melodic ascent to depict the storm coming nearer, and then descent, as if to depict the sounds of heavy winds and rainfall dropping to the ground.

Vivaldi and Bach use melody, harmony, and rhythm as *invitations* to experience the world in a very particular way, and thus to *share* in an experience indicative of a larger lifeworld. These are musical gestures

---

speculated that Vivaldi himself may have written it. Regardless, it is widely accepted that the sonnets help us interpret the detailed nuances of the concertos.

and forms that not only exemplify a world of order and loveliness, but that also invite us to *delight in* creation, to *love* that world of order and loveliness, and thus conform our loves to God's economy of goods.

However, few composers have impacted my students as powerfully and profoundly as the Estonian composer Arvo Pärt, considered by many to be the greatest living composer. Beloved by rock stars, film producers, and documentary makers, his music comprises perhaps the single most sought after sounds floating across the borders of classical music today. Once known for atonal, avant-garde, and serialist musical compositions, Pärt went silent for almost ten years. It was during this time that he converted to Russian Orthodoxy and began studying in-depth the techniques and processes of early Christian music, particularly the unadorned melodic contours of plainchant, or what's more popularly known as Gregorian Chant.

He then began experimenting with the sounds awakening from the intertwining of two melodic voices, which in turn became an Incarnational-model for the whole of his subsequent works: a melody line that captures the adversities and struggles of this fallen world, and a melodic counterpoint of divine grace and healing that redeems and transfigures the pains and sorrows of our world. Arvo Pärt's decade-long silence involved nothing less than his own return to a world filled with divine meaning and purpose, from which he forged a compositional technique that sonically reanimated that mystical world into our own, awakening us to the divine reality that surrounds us and yet remains eclipsed by the assumptions of a secular age.

Pärt called this new-ancient style of composition 'tintinnabuli,' which means literally 'the sound of a small bell.' And with good reason; his music seems to mystically cascade from inside the purity of overtones resounding in such ringing. Central to this compositional technique is Pärt's use of silence and space, which transform into the mystical canvas upon which his music floats.

Pärt himself describes it this way:

> Time, for us, is like the time of our own lives. It is temporary. What is timeless is the time of eternal life; that is eternal. Like the sun, we cannot really look at it directly, but my intuition tells me that the human soul is closely connected to both of the them, time and eternity.[29]

When listening to his music, you'll hear that Pärt often ends his phrases in a dissonance, without completed resolution; this compositional technique for Pärt represents the sins of humanity, which have distorted the world around us. And yet, this dissonance is interwoven with melodies of divine grace and mercy, thus transfiguring his music into a sonic revelation of the incorporation of the entire cosmos into the transformative life, death, and resurrection of Christ.

The soundscape created by Arvo Pärt draws the listener into the rich and illustrious world of Russian Orthodox music, and as such, recovers the sacramental and indeed mystical nature of art and beauty. Far from our world's consumerist sensibilities, that render music and art to a matter of mere personal preference and subjective taste, art and beauty were once considered bridges to another world, indeed, an eternal world that has broken into our own through the Incarnation of Christ and the restoration of the cosmos. Arvo Pärt's music invites us to reimagine our world in just such a way, wherein our desires are drawn towards heaven, into a divine communion, in which all things are eternally perfected in God.

---

29. Tom Huizenga, "The Silence And Awe Of Arvo Pärt," *Morning Edition*, June 2, 2014, accessed April 4, 2019, http://www.npr.org/

CONCLUSION

The significant challenge facing classical educators today is teaching students to understand music as a mediator between the objective physics of the cosmos on the one hand and the human soul on the other. For the classical civilizations of the Greeks, Jews, and Christians, the revelatory significance of music involved manifesting on earth the music of the heavens, that is, the mathematical symmetries and consonances that constitute a harmonious cosmos. For the Greeks in particular, music resounded the mathematical principles of perfection upon which the cosmos was modeled. And in the Jewish temple, sacred music invoked the presence of God, the Lord of heaven and earth. Early Christians drew from both Greek and Jewish traditions in the formation of their own music theory and practice that understood the music of the church as revelatory of the reunification of heaven and earth in the transformative life, death, and resurrection of Christ.

Specifically, it is through melodic, harmonic, and rhythmic gestures that music invites the affections and sensibilities of the human person to delight in and indeed align with the divine economy of goods embedded in the harmonies of the cosmos. The acoustic revelation of divine meaning and purpose served to cultivate wisdom and virtue within the listener, who through music participated in the harmony of the cosmos and thus became truly human. For the Pythagorean tradition, the link between sound and mathematics provided the means by which the music of the spheres, otherwise imperceptible, could be reproduced on earth, transforming its listeners into heavenly beings.

This classical vision of music stands in stark contrast to the contemporary notion of pop music, which substitutes an emphasis on objective form with an appeal to the movement of the body, rendering

---

sections/deceptivecadence/2014/06/02/316322238/the-silence-and-awe-of-arvo-p-rt.

rock'n'roll particularly vulnerable to aesthetic and moral relativism. Because rock music emphasizes subjective appeal over objective form, it tends to lack the formative resources necessary to shape and cultivate our humanity in accordance with wisdom and virtue. The classical notion of *ordo amoris* or right ordering of our loves provides a model by which the student can learn the value of the formative significance of classical music while at the same time providing room for the continued enjoyment of contemporary pop music, thus providing the student with a distinctively classical approach to musical enrichment and education.

2

CLASSICAL *vs.* PROGRESSIVE EDUCATION

DAVID GOODWIN

To embark on our journey toward the true, good, and beautiful, we need to take the rocks out of our packs put there by those jokers who run the other education camp. This is particularly true regarding music and the arts. Most of us grew up in John Dewey's progressive schools, not in classical Christian schools. In movies we see progressive schools portrayed as the accepted standard. Nearly everyone we know attended one of them. Because of this, our mental models for music education are often steeped with progressive influence. This influence is especially intertwined with music educators who were trained in the progressive model. While most other subjects have completely abandoned classical thinking, music has maintained some classical sensibilities about training, making the separation of baby and bathwater quite difficult.

PROGRESSIVE SCHOOL HISTORY

Progressive education began with roots in Rousseau, Pestalozzi, and Fröbel, for the most part, between 1905 and 1915. High schools as we know them today were invented at this time. The invention of 50-minute "carnegie" units, seven-period days with students moving between classrooms were standardized at this time, as well as classroom sizes, bells, and the general subjects taught today. With the rise of the industrial revolution came the decline of the outdated vestiges of the past—faith, art, architecture, and more. The excitement of new inventions and industrialization of society dampened the country's motivation to build on the past. Against this backdrop, during the '20s, '30s, and '40s, progressive education boomed during the era of big band music. Not surprisingly, school music programs were heavily influenced by this trend and pushed the evolution of their music programs into bands and glee clubs. Wars and sports brought bands onto the marching field. In the late '40s and '50s, as the cast from the progressive smelter cooled, school music became a thing unto itself. School bands, choirs, and glee clubs were ensconced and the industry that surrounds school music was born.

New composers in this era sought to reinforce the latest social norms being taught in education. This meant that their music compositions were focused not on what had come before, but on what was fresh and popular. The booming music industry thrived under this goal because school music programs would buy, perform, and buy again, always looking for the latest musical novelty. An endless stream of sheet music was designed to make a profit while also paralleling the changes that progressive education was bringing to society. The grammar schools were affected as well. This school music industry cycle was further propagated by festivals and competitions that more and more valued the new and trendy over the tried and tested. And, of course, most music education degrees, as offered by education departments partnered with music departments, were informed by this pattern of new music. Where previous generations of educators surveyed and studied the best music from centuries past, progressive educators sought to move forward with no regard for the past. Now there are countless pieces for band, choir, and orchestra that rose to prominence, thanks to progressive education.

With the rise of marching bands and pep bands, orchestras became rare in progressive schools unless the school was large. School athletics were the catalyst for this change. It may not be easy to march with a cello on the fifty-yard line nor is it an instrument that amplifies all the way to the crowd, but the prominence of band ensembles over string ensembles was not solely practical. Orchestra music was considered a relic of a bygone era. Art music, or what many generally refer to as classical music, is more associated with the string orchestra than the brass and woodwind of the marching band. In addition, the types of music desired on the sidelines were much less demanding than what was needed in the orchestra pit. In any case, strings were secondary, and the horn and band took the lead.

What then is progressive music education? Actually, it is not entirely progressive. Some areas of change in the progressive education system were highly purposeful—like the reworking of humanities into social studies. But music seems to have holed up as a vestige of the semi-traditional education model within the progressive system. We can take some good from it, like opportunities to participate in the resulting festivals, but that does not mean that progressive music education is a good thing. Nor is it a harmless thing. As evidenced by nearly everything that classical education is trying to recover, the great harm inflicted by progressive education is not the result of what its proponents did, but what they removed.

Before we examine what was removed, one more often overlooked consequence from progressive school music should concern us. Since the 1980s, church music also changed as progressive education became the standard. Specifically, the rise of the worship band brought in a new model for Christian schools to emulate. Now a handful of students on instruments borrowed from the folk and rock and roll genres lead worship for school assemblies. This can lead a school culture to an inadvertent emphasis on this type of popular church music at the exclusion of knowing the historical music style and practices of the church. We may differ on whether this style of worship is a good thing, but it inevitably pushes out something else.

In so much of progressive education, the traditions it replaces represent a substantial loss. Historically, education was aligned with church music. Many classical Christian schools were church schools with a choirmaster who taught the students Latin in addition to choir. This made vocal music an anchor. The students were practiced in canticles and psalm settings that were hundreds, if not thousands of years old. These forms of music provided a much deeper study of beauty and training than what can be gleaned by studying only new settings of music, instilling in our studentsa rooted, historic affection for what is beautiful.

PROGRESSIVE ERRORS

There are three erroneous progressive principles that get in the way of our recovery of what was lost. These are the things that push out something else. Progressives teach that beauty is subjective, that music is without higher or lower purpose, and that students are simply containers to be filled, rather than souls to be nurtured toward virtue. We will address each of these.

1. *Beauty in Art and Music are Subjective*

Others in this book have addressed this, but I will briefly mention it here because it has wide-ranging implications for your school. We need to consider and unpack this claim. "Subjective" means that the truth, goodness, and beauty of something is in the eye of the beholder—or the subject who is viewing it. To be "subjective" means that they cannot be "objective." These are mutually exclusive terms. To be "objective" means that the value of something is intrinsic within the object (artifact, song, or the performance). How can this be? How can a thing have intrinsic value outside of what humans assign to it? Because any object's goodness, truthfulness, and beauty is measured on a transcendent measuring scale—God's measuring scale. It has fixed value in the divine realm, independent of what value we give it here in our temporal world.

A violin concerto by J.S. Bach reveals beauty in a way that can be objectively recognized without consulting the feelings of the listener or the composer's intent. It is beautiful insofar as God, The Listener, places an absolute measuring stick next to it. Plato taught that any musical song we create is a dim reflection of some divine ideal song. This is because "ideal" or "perfect" can only exist in God.

Sometimes I ask Christians who argue against objectivity in art or music to do a thought experiment: "What if you think that song is beautiful but God does not?" I usually hear something like "God doesn't hate anything—especially art or music. He loves us, so he loves everything we create!" It is not difficult at this point to conjure up a pile of reprehensible art made in recent decades. A quick trip through Deuteronomy also dispels this argument. What about specific directions for the art in the temple? Or God's hatred, not just of false gods, but of the graven images people created to reflect them? I usually ask one more question: "If you think God does not have tastes or preferences, where do your tastes come from? Do you have affections that God does not? Wouldn't that make you greater than God in some respect?" And then I ask again, "Is it OK to have tastes that conflict with God's?" We can conclude that every object has a purpose and God has an affection or disaffection for it. Whatever we do in our classrooms, we must train students that music, like all of creation, has objective value rooted in measurements put forth by God.

2. Music is Without Higher or Lower Purpose

Progressives believe that the purpose of music is incidental and unrelated to its beauty. Everything is considered flat, equal, and purposeless, and things only earn token value by preference or usefulness. Classical Christian educators know that music is high or low in purpose, and matched either with excellence or mediocrity to that purpose. These two dimensions define every piece of music. Why is one type of music better than another for worship? Or for street musicians? Or for cattle drives? Or for classical Christian educators with an aim at absolute truth, goodness, and beauty? We know that God is purposeful in all that he does. Purpose, both in a Christian sense and a classical sense, creates the context for beauty and complexity.

For example, progressives might argue that a presidential inauguration could have any type of music and be equally presidential, especially if the music is what the individual person (the president elect) prefers. This idea would have been absurd to the classical mind. The president's inauguration should not be about the individual, but about the office. This requires a certain type of music suitable to the purpose. Orchestrated, high music should define the ceremony, not the president's favorite blues tune.[1]

Before the middle of the 18th century, musicians strove to conform to this understanding of high and low purpose to music. They were not merely to express themselves, but they sought to interact with the sublime or even express it. Music was written in a style not only that sought to fully complement its intended function, but also that sought

---

1. See C.S. Lewis' passage on "Solemnity" from his preface to *Paradise Lost*.

to do so in subjection to the Creator who made all things. Music and lyrics were to uphold one another throughout a song. Whether for church, ceremony, ball, or a pub, the function determined the style and form of the piece. Church and ceremonial music were higher styles with levels of glory and meaning not present in lower styles like folk or pub music.[2] Both had a place. But the system and worldview that directed the artist began to change. The interconnectedness of form and content with function was reduced to mere utility, devoid of submission to anyone outside the hearer.

3. *Students are Simply Containers to be Filled*

Since progressives do not recognize the transcendent, they cannot appreciate the goal of shaping children to an image outside of themselves, one that is that is higher and better. Often we hear the refrain "You're great just the way you are." Christians have absorbed this idea as well—"God loves you just the way you are." Repentance and transformation, though central themes of the gospel, are minimized.

Though there is great reward in aligning our souls with higher truth, goodness, and beauty, the work required to attain it is also great. Cultivation of truth, goodness and beauty results in an affection and appreciation for great music. The question is Augustinian: Are our affections aligned with God's? Augustine puts it this way:

> [The virtuous man] keeps his affections also under
> strict control, so that he neither loves what he ought
> not to love, nor fails to love what he ought to love,

---

2. It is often said that Luther obtained the melodies for his hymns from bar songs. A Lutheran theologian told me this is a myth, connected with a poor translation of the word 'bar.' Certainly, some hymns, like "We Gather Together" bear resemblance to pub songs at the time. But which came from which? Most evidence indicates that high church music was made for that purpose and led the culture.

nor loves that equally which ought to be loved either less or more, nor loves less or more which ought to be loved equally.[3]

As classical Christian educators, we are concerned with cultivating rightly ordered affections in our students. Our music programs should be informed by this purpose. Notice the language above: "strict control." Our task is to train students vigorously to love what they ought. With a little help, they will appreciate higher things. But if we give them only what they naturally love, they will in the old-world sense remain vulgar.

CONCLUSION

While society's understanding today about music education has maintained some paltry sensibilities, the overall scene is a trainwreck. Again, the great harm from the progressives is not in what they did, but in what they removed. Out go the objective standards, the purpose, and the soul-shaping power of music. If we are careful as educators to guard against these errors, our journey along with our students towards the true, good, and beautiful will be all the easier for the extra baggage removed from our packs. Here's to being progressive, in the classical sense.

---

3. Augustine, "The Order of Love" in *The City of God*, Chapter 27.

3

TAKE EVERYTHING CAPTIVE *to* CHRIST

KENT YOUNG

Understanding the implications of Christ's supremacy in any endeavor is a daunting task. It is the task of discipleship and takes a lifetime. In the music classroom, the Lordship of Christ shapes everything from what is taught to the manner of instruction. It has implications for everything from the purpose of a concert to the purpose of training in literacy. It means that every classroom moment from the first greeting to the final benediction is pregnant with meaning and purpose. A Christian music program will seek to glorify Christ and train up the next generation of disciples.

CHRIST IS THE OBJECTIVE STANDARD

Viewed from the side, as in the case of a concert or a one-off visit to a classroom, it would be difficult to recognize the difference between an excellent classical Christian music program and any other excellent music program. In the concert, one would expect to hear beautiful music performed skillfully by students who are engaged and engaging. In the classroom, one might expect to see students engaged in a delightful and rigorous program of music literacy or analysis. The similarities will be substantial because there really is only one way to cultivate excellence in music whether you are a Christian or not. No music pedagogue who holds to a radically relativistic view of truth, goodness, and beauty has ever produced an excellent music program by obeying their own principles. Excellent music is a reflection of an objective reality regardless of any inner conviction on the part of the one making it.

Furthermore, music as a discipline has the added advantage of a kind of aesthetic immediacy by which to make qualitative judgments. When a child is learning to play the violin, it is quite easy to tell whether or not he has practiced since his last lesson. The violin does not lie. I suspect this is why many music programs have retained a classical pedagogy, even while other subjects have abandoned it. It is true that there have been many modern schools that have adopted a kind of free expression, or music appreciation model of music education. But it will be immediately apparent that this pedagogy does not work when the students of these programs open their mouths to sing. What works and has always worked is a more classical model of education where students are taught the grammar, logic, and rhetoric of music.

All excellent music programs will, to one extent or other, be structured this way—the classical way. The immediate, experiential nature of music causes us to acknowledge, sometimes against our own will, that there is an objective standard for beauty. The classical mind willfully acknowledges this fact. While the nature of the objective standard may have varied greatly—everything from the cosmos to various deities—the objectivity of the standard meant that it existed quite apart from human assessment. Man could either discover and participate, in the standard, or not. To the extent that he did participate he became more human and understood more about his world. This is the fundamental bent of the classical mind, and therefore, of classical education.

The foundation and objective standard for Classical Christian education is Christ Himself.[1] Classical Christian education begins with the notion that all things were made by Him, through Him, and for Him, and in Him all things have their being. This fundamental reality requires us to reorient every aspect of our instruction. We know, for instance, that the education of the child is the God-given responsibility of the parents, and more specifically the fathers.[2] We can therefore say that the school is an extension of the family. This will have many implications for our program, not least of which will be our duty to communicate with parents and seek their help as we seek to help them. But this is only one example. The point is that a Christian music program will seek to understand what it means to instruct under the Lordship of Christ at all levels and in all things.

SIN IS THE BIGGEST HURDLE

While acknowledging that truth, goodness, and beauty are universal and timeless, it is important to keep in mind that our classrooms are situated in a certain time and place. We must recognize we are teaching within the context of a prevailing culture that shapes the presuppositions and habits of thought of our students. We need to know which idols our students are going to be tempted to worship, the lies they are going to be told, and the sins toward which they will be most tempted. And we need to recognize that we are situated within the same culture and are prone to the same temptations.

---

1. Colossians 1:17; John 1.

2. Deuteronomy 6; Ephesians 6:4; Colossians 3:21; Proverbs 4:1-4.

The most pernicious idol we face today is the idol of Self-Identity. Self-Identity is the notion that I get to choose my identity. I get to make myself, define who I am and what it means to be me. This idol has been with us a long time. Even before Disney began writing songs about discontented princesses wanting more from their world, we were a country of self-made men. But in our current cultural milieu this idol has finally shown its face. Whereas in former generations, Self-Identity was the ability to choose between being a butcher, baker, or candlestick maker, today we are told we can choose our gender. We now commonly say that truth is open to interpretation. The prevailing culture in which we live has lost any common standard by which to evaluate the world around us precisely because we want each individual to have the prerogative of a god, or rather we want that prerogative for ourselves. Self-Identity stands juxtaposed to the foundational principle on which a Christian education is built. Therefore our efforts at building a Christian music program will often be an exercise in combating this idol.

The supremacy of Christ is a question of authority. When we acknowledge Christ's lordship, all things get reordered, from our identity to the purpose of singing. The first thing we will realize is that our biggest problem is the sinfulness of man. Hopefully we will realize our own sinfulness and begin there. Our sinfulness—the sinfulness of man—cannot be glossed over in a Christian music program. If we are going to have an excellent music program under the lordship of Christ, we must become adept at dealing with sin and training our students to do the same.

Eighteen years of teaching choirs has taught me something: a choir that is out of fellowship with one another or with God has a hard time making beautiful music. It is hard to sing praises to God, or for that matter psalms and hymns that are rich in theological truths, when we are in sin. It is equally difficult making harmony with our neighbor if our relationship with them is out of joint. Any school that meets

180 days a year is bound to have problems with sin. It is unavoidable. It is not a matter of if, but a matter of when. For music teachers, it is difficult to give up precious class time to deal with sinful students. We often do not have as much class time as we would like, and the concert is always looming. But we must recognize two things. First, it is our first duty of Christian love to restore sinning students to fellowship.[3] Second, the time we take to deal with sin in our classroom will result in blessing for the time we have left to instruct in music. In time this will reap benefits far beyond musical skill.

It is far easier to detect sin in grammar classes than in the secondary. Younger students simply do not have the sophistication to hide their sin. I have also noticed that it is easier to detect when adolescent boys are out of fellowship than adolescent girls. I am convinced this is also a matter of sophistication. Boys are more likely than girls to simply have it out in public. In any case, fellowship must be won before music can be made. We cannot always know what specific sins our students are battling. When we do, we ought to deal with those sins specifically. But singing provides us with a barometer for the overall state of our students.

Several years ago I began a practice that had the unintentional consequence of helping me address fellowship in my classes. I began using a sung greeting—a kind of call and response to begin class. When students enter class I sing something like, "Praise the Lord!" They respond in four parts with, "Praise the Lord, O my soul!" From that one greeting I can quickly get a sense of the state of the student fellowship. If they are out of sorts, it is immediately apparent. The question to explore next is "why?" In the middle of January, it may be that they are tired of cold air, school, and one another. It may be that the majority of them are dealing with sickness. Or it may be that there is some kind of drama between students. Whatever the case, I am able

---

3. Galatians 6:1-2.

to attend to the state of my students and ask God to reveal where I can help them. Because these greetings are in the imperative mood, taken from the Psalms, the text is a springboard to encourage students to attend to the state of their souls. If they find that they are grumbling in their spirits, angry with their neighbor, whatever the trouble, the imperative, "Praise the Lord, O my soul!" is a good word to themselves. It is a good word provided they are heeding the command. As with all of us, students can easily sing without attending to the words they are saying. As Christian music teachers, it is our job to call their attention to the text. I have found on many occasions that when I take the time to remind students of what they are singing and its significance, they will respond with confession of sin. When sin is taken care of, joy in singing follows.

BUILD A CORPUS OF SONG

The Psalms contain many more imperatives. Psalm 42 and 43 are great examples. The Psalmist asks himself, "Why are you cast down, O my soul?" The antidote is a few lines later, "Hope in God!" In the Psalms God gives us a vocabulary to speak encouragement and admonishment to ourselves and to others. We are commanded in Ephesians 5:19 (New King James Version) to be "filled with the Spirit, speaking to one another in psalms and hymns and spiritual songs." This command is given in the context of walking in wisdom as one who redeems the time. The parallel passage in Colossians 3:16 teaches us that singing these songs to one another is how the word of Christ dwells in us richly. When we sing psalms and hymns and spiritual songs, we are in fact teaching and admonishing one another.

If we desire the word of Christ to dwell richly in our students, we need to give them a corpus of song heavy in the Psalms and rich in Christ's word. We want them to have a large corpus to draw upon in order to express the range of human experience and emotion as they seek to walk in the Spirit and grow in wisdom and stature. As students sing these songs again and again they memorize them and hide them in their hearts. Music powerfully informs them how they ought to feel about a particular text. It also provides a sense of formal structure through which to imagine the text and more easily memorize it. The rhythms and melodies are a delight and lend themselves to repetition that is rarely tiresome. When students participate in singing, the music confirms and rehearses the text for them. Over the course of several years, this confirming and rehearsing of the word of Christ causes it to dwell in our students' hearts richly. When they need comfort, rebuke, or words to express gratitude or praise, their hearts are a storehouse ready to render up fitting words.

The task of developing and implementing a corpus of song is not the task of a single day, or even a year. Many of us have never sung the Psalms, and even if we have, many of our students will have had little exposure to the texts or music of historic psalmody. The situation is tricky at best. Ultimately, we want our students to love God's song book. If we introduce a heap of songs that are unfamiliar in their text and musical aesthetic, we will have a mess on our hands quickly. We have to keep in mind simultaneously the trajectory of our institution and our students. The questions we have to ask are, "How much capital do I have with my students? How uncomfortable are they, and is it sustainable?" When the current kindergarten students are seniors, the answer to those questions will change considerably. They will have been shaped by the culture you have established and will not find it irksome.

I would suggest beginning with songs that are easily accessible. Our first steps need to be just at the edges of the cultural milieu of our students. If they are being fed on popular music and praise choruses, the first songs we give them ought to be within reach of that context. Begin with songs that are in a rounded binary form, are either in a major or minor mode, and have a regular meter. Now is not the time for church modes and mixed meter. I would suggest songs in the key of E flat major or G major to begin. I would also suggest songs that are devotional in nature. Songs that are heavy in theology or songs of lament will tend to tempt students to complain. A good example of a song to begin might be "Be Thou My Vision," "The King of Love (Psalm 23)," or "Holy, Holy, Holy."

We want to make sure we meet our students where they are, and that we take them where they ought to be. Once the students are singing three or four songs well, it may be time to introduce a song that stretches them a bit musically and theologically. The fact that they now have some songs they can sing well and look forward to singing will give you enough capital to push them a bit with the next song. You will find that they are soon willing to work through the difficulties of a song that is outside their cultural experience and stretches their understanding with a lot more joy and energy.

This process of building a corpus of song can take several years, but it is worth every moment. I have found that three or four songs a year, outside of concert repertoire, is a good pace for keeping energy and enthusiasm up through the process. Remember that even if the first graduating class only learns a handful of songs, they will have a handful more than they would have otherwise possessed. By the time the kindergarten class is seniors, they will be able to sing between sixty and seventy psalms and hymns. And most likely, if you are diligent in singing these songs regularly, they will have most of them memorized.

One of the greatest blessings of teaching students who are filled with psalms and hymns is that you have a cultural vocabulary from which to draw while dealing with daily life in the school. The psalms especially give us words to describe sin, pain, joy, faith, loss, despair, and all manner of human experience. They also teach us how to think well and live faithfully in the midst of these experiences. Singing great psalms and hymns regularly is tantamount to rehearsing the word of

Christ. When we sing, the music fixes the text in our memory while informing and confirming how we ought to feel about the text we are singing.

And this, incidentally, is perhaps the best apologetic for teaching music literacy. If we are able to give our students seventy songs, they will possess seventy songs and an appreciation for those songs. But if we teach them to read music, then the whole storehouse of psalms and hymns is open to them. They will be able to sing the whole psalter. The simple reading and recitation of the word of Christ will be elevated in the joyous discovery of beautiful tunes that adorn the words of life.

SINGING IN THE CRACKS

The shaping power of music has long been a topic of discussion, if not debate. Since Plato and Aristotle at least, the topic of music's power to shape human persons and culture has been a hotbed of conversation. Everything from the power of particular modes to the danger of certain kinds of songs has been contemplated and discussed. A good book that discusses some of the thinking of the early church fathers on the subject of music is Calvin Stapert's *A New Song for an Old World: Musical Thought in the Early Church*. In it Stapert explores the writings of several church fathers, from Clement of Alexandria to Saint John Chrysostom, on the power of music. While it is clear that there was very little in the way of systematic thought regarding the power of music, Stapert concludes, rightly I believe, that music is a powerful gift which can be either pernicious or beneficial. Stapert commends, as did the church fathers, the regular singing of psalms and hymns in our corporate and devotional lives. He says, "We need to teach them to our children and find ways and occasions to use them regularly."[4]

---

4. Calvin R. Stapert, *A New Song for an Old World: Musical Thought in the Early Church* (Grand Rapids: Eerdmans, 2007), 194.

We know from our own experience that music is a powerful part of culture. It confirms and rehearses our cultural assumptions. A Christian music program will seek to not simply subvert pernicious musical influences, but to encourage beneficial ones. It will seek to supplant the cultural soundtrack with songs that confirm and rehearse godly virtue. There are several opportunities throughout the school day to pause and sing songs that give thanks to God, orient our minds rightly to the task ahead, or ask for God's grace and guidance as we begin. I call this "singing in the cracks."

I mentioned before that we began singing our greetings before class. Many of these greetings are a call and response intended to focus the students' minds on the task of praising God. We also sing a lunch blessing with all of the secondary before heading off to eat. This blessing was written to give thanks, ask God's blessing on the food, and recall the students to their unity in Christ and duty to live out that unity through fellowship at lunch. Beginning class with a psalm or hymn chosen for a text that connects with a lesson is another way to allow music to shape the culture and students at a school.

Singing in the cracks does not have to be disruptive. Every school has rhythms and events that constitute the warp and woof of the school. Thesis presentations, graduation, balls, sporting events, conferences, recitations, special meals, protocol, before and after vacations, and even the beginning and ending of the day or week are all pregnant moments that lend themselves beautifully to a song that can interpret the meaning of the moment for our students. Beginning and ending these events with a carefully chosen song, or better yet, a specially composed song, will have a shaping power that cannot be easily defined, but will surely be experienced. It will shape the experience of the event by defining how students ought to regard the event or how they ought to respond to it. A basketball team that ends a game by singing the doxology will begin to understand that the fitting response to a well fought competition between brothers or sisters in Christ is the praise of the Most High. A school day that begins by singing about God's new mercies will begin with students who are rightly oriented to the reality of the day.

But the shaping power of singing in the cracks will not be automatic. Instruction, encouragement, and frequent reminders are a must if students are to attend to these songs with understanding and interest. Specific application of song texts will help students to see these songs are not simply a churchy add-on, but rather a sincere expression of truth in the moment. A good teacher will remind students that they are to sing with their spirits and with their understanding (1 Cor. 14:15).

SINGING AGAINST THE GRAIN

If we do our job faithfully, we can expect push back. We live in a world that is hostile to Christ and His church. The world cannot countenance the notion that there is such a thing as objective truth, goodness, or beauty. Christian music teachers seeking to build a classical Christian music program must train students to evaluate music in light of an objective standard of beauty. The notion that beauty is in the eye of the beholder is such an intertwined cultural assumption, it is invisible to all but the most thoughtful observer. The battle over objective standards of beauty will arise at every possible instance from questions over choice of concert repertoire, choice of music for the ball, and most certainly when a teacher seeks to teach psalms and hymns. Objections will come most often from students in the logic and rhetoric stages. But they will also come from parents, administrators, other teachers, and even grammar students. Christian music teachers must be prepared for these objections.

Rightly understood, opposition is an opportunity to teach and shape those who are doing the opposing. When opposition arises, it is difficult to keep cool, especially when the objection is over a piece of music you have carefully chosen or a criticism of the kinds of pieces you select generally. In these moments a Christian music teacher must keep in mind that the student in front of them bears the image of God. Their objection is only possible because they are an image bearer. The value of the child far exceeds the value of any song. The task before us is not to commend or condemn a song for the sake of the song, but for the sake of the child. I have found that listening carefully to a student's objection and helping them clarify their position results in the double blessing of gaining capital with the student and helping them form categories of thought that are consistent with the notion that beauty is objective. If we are perceived as terse and dogmatic in our assessments, we will quickly lose the trust of our students, their parents, and our colleagues.

While beauty is objective, it is not, at least in creation, absolute. There are kinds of beauty and degrees of beauty. Our job is to open our students' understanding to varieties of song and help them understand the notion of fittingness. Many students will not understand, for instance, why singing a Beatles song in the midst of a concert comprised of psalms might not be fitting. A Christian music teacher will train students to wrestle with questions such as the fittingness or merit of a particular song with Christ as Lord of all and the objective standard of beauty. Train them to attend to various aesthetic features of the song and evaluate it accordingly. Help them evaluate the quality and truth of the text as well as the marriage of the text and music, and give them the categories of thought that will allow them to evaluate the fittingness of particular songs in particular situations.

I have, on several occasions, asked my older students to bring in a favorite song to present to the class. My goal was for them to describe why the song was compelling. This exercise requires a lot of preparation and many guard rails. But if done well it allows students to wrestle with ideas of fittingness, quality, and beauty using music that is familiar. To prepare for this exercise I taught several lessons outlining categories of evaluation. These categories can range from melodic analysis to formal analysis. The important thing is to limit them to a few categories so they can focus their attention and make quality judgments. The end goal, however, is not to train students to be placid academics, but to be rigorous thinkers. We want students who insist that beauty is an attribute of God and therefore objective. Furthermore, we want beauty, as an attribute of God, to be more intelligible to our students so they will know and love God with all of their mind, soul, and strength.

SINGING AND TAKING STOCK

We desire these things for our students because we love our students. As Christian music teachers we recognize that our students are bearers of God's image and will live forever. By God's grace we will sing with them for eternity. As those who love music, music teachers are tempted to sacrifice students to the idol of excellent music. We ought to insist upon excellent music because the dignity of image-bearers requires nothing less, and God's glory demands our best. But we must recognize that the choices we make about the structure of our music program ought to be reflective of our love for our students as well as our love for our subject.

Our love for our students will be evident in our choices regarding repertoire, pacing, and timing—among other things. Our choices of literature will reflect a desire for our students both to stretch and grow and to be culturally engaged. If we insist on singing medieval organum, we can expect them to revolt. If we choose Michael Jackson, we can expect them to suspect us. We ought to have enough respect for them as image bearers to be able to appreciate songs that stretch their capacities—both instrumentally and intellectually—and yet bear with their frame. Their frame has, in some part, to do with the cultural milieu in which they are being raised. We cannot expect those who cut their teeth on pop music and praise songs to be immediately enamored with Mendelssohn or Bach. The encouraging part is that with the growth of a singing culture within a school, students will begin to desire better and better literature.

However, no matter their position in this process, we must insist on good literature. This does not mean the most difficult or lofty literature. We do not expect 6th graders to read Augustine's *Confessions*. We do, however, expect our upper class students to give it a try. But even there we do not expect them to engage in the kinds of discussion we would have with our colleagues over the same material. The same is true for music. We ought to find quality literature that is good and fits the frame of our students. There are wonderful songs that are simple enough for kindergarten students to sing. These point forward to Bach and Mendelssohn.

As for pacing, this is a matter of wisdom and observation. The key here is paying attention to what the students are communicating. It is difficult and takes a lot of humility to bend our will such that we are not over stretching our students. We want academic excellence. We want students who learn to love what we love. Too often we are willing to put *Veggie Tales* on for our toddlers, then expect our Rhetoric aged children to listen in rapt attention to Bach's *St. Matthew Passion*. In the first place, we need to remember that we are partnering with parents who do not always get what it is we are doing. If a student's parent still plays Huey Lewis and the News, we can not expect their child to take to Bach in the first instance. We need to recognize that we are building a culture in which these students will marinate for many years. This culture, if done with patience and in faith, will ruin them for Huey. They will grow in their capacities to love good poetry and the music that best expresses it. We ought to have a vision that expands beyond the year, the decade, and our career. But the difficult task is understanding where we are in the trajectory of that vision. The best way forward is to simply get moving and constantly take stock. Adjustments will need to be made almost constantly for pacing.

Our timing is related to our pacing. As music educators we ought to be in tune with the capacities of our students. We need to know what they can do, and introduce literature that is just outside of our students' current abilities. This gives us the ability to stretch their capacities just enough for them to experience success with the literature we have chosen for them to do. This ought to be done with careful notice of their current loves and abilities. John Milton Gregory's *The Seven Laws of Teaching* is helpful in this regard. His fifth law states, "The truth to be taught must be learned in through truth already known."[5] As educators, we cannot teach rightly until we have learned something about the capacities of our students.

As we build classical Christian music programs, we need to keep the main things central. Christ is Lord over all things, including music education. We are teaching image-bearers who will one day be parents, churchmen, and ultimately a royal priesthood and citizens of the kingdom of heaven. A Christian music program will insist on excellence and beauty, but will keep a sense of proportion recognizing that we have been called to teach particular students at a particular time in a particular place. God will bless our work according to His grace and mercy. Our job is to faithfully work out what it means to teach music under the authority of Christ.

---

5. John Milton Gregory, *The Seven Laws of Teaching* (Lancaster: Veritas Press, 2004), 83.

SECTION TWO

PRACTICE

4

The SINGING SCHOOL

A Classical Christian School Music Program

JARROD RICHEY

Schola cantorum is a common name for college and university choirs across the country. It means a "Singing School." When I first encountered the Latin phrase, I did not find it being used in the music education program at a classical Christian school but by a college choir. And yet it would be hard to find a more succinct Latin phrase that describes the musical aim at a classical Christian school. A *Schola cantorum*, or Singing School, is an essential part of training the next generation to make melody to the Lord with all the benefits that come from that.[1]

---

1. Ephesians 5:19.

THE TUNEFUL CAMPUS

Imagine the difference a Singing School could make at your campus. What sounds would a prospective student's family hear while touring the school? Is the school quietly reverent and serious? Or is walking into the school like walking outside and enjoying God's creation, full of bird songs and clashing pitches, rhythms and rhymes? If the school is a *Schola cantorum*, identified by that feature, singing will be heard throughout each school day, all across the campus. The door to the choir room, or band room, will not be the only boisterous spot in the hallways.

The appropriate time to set the tone as a Singing School is when students and faculty gather and start the school day together in chapel or a more general assembly. There are so many ways to raise voices together at this time. A few options might include a school hymn that everyone knows by heart, perhaps a liturgy of musical calls and responses, or even a sung greeting and ending blessing. Since our scriptural call as Christians is to present our bodies as sacrifices of praise, what better way to demonstrate this priority than by the singing in chapels and convocations during the week.[2] We must make sure our students understand a classical Christian school is not neutral about singing. They are image bearers of a singing God and should recognize this truth from its prevalence in their school culture.[3]

If the prospective student's family is still touring the school, they would be sure to hear singing from the classrooms. A Singing School starts with its youngest learners. They are memorizing great mountains of information. Songs and jingles and rhymes make this task bite-sized and fun. A young student would happily chant through the names of the continents for a visiting stranger. Look for those resources that

---

2. Romans 12:1.

3. Zephaniah 3:17.

help our little ones memorize and rehearse the facts studied during the grammar stage of the *Trivium* through song. History chants, Latin jingles, or recognizing an adult with a melodic greeting are some of the features of a singing school's classroom. As might be apparent by now, the music teacher is not the only one feeding the school's music culture.

A Singing School also will encourage its students to sing in less formal times of fellowship and togetherness. Lunch-time gatherings or end-of-day clean-up make excellent opportunities for more singing. At my school, for example, students of the logic and rhetoric stages of the *Trivium* will often break into song while finishing an art assignment or when they have completed their work at the end of a study hall period. A love of singing together should slowly become comfortable and normal to the students. Such moments show anyone listening that music is seeping into the school's cultural fabric.

THE MUSIC MANDATE

The hallmark of any school wanting to build up a musical culture and the ability of its students is the institution's treatment of musical courses as requirements, not electives.

A couple of "musts" feed this principle.

Theologically, because singing is something God calls the church to do in imitation of Himself, Christians *must* obey Him, especially while training the next generation. We are training worshippers in the kingdom of God. They *must* sing with the understanding described in Psalm 47:7. God set forth singing as a creational pattern that we must echo, again and again.

Practically, because music is a difficult language, students *must* be immersed in it from their youngest years to obtain a useful mastery by the time they graduate. The immersion is formal and informal but combines to give students the ability to speak, read, and write in the language of music. If music instruction and singing are left to an elective class, the remarkable fruit of true music literacy will be stagnant and never escape infancy.

THE AIM AT MASTERY

Continuing with the comparison of music to language, formal instruction and training of musically literate students easily tracks with common practices used to teach the English language. Students start by writing their letters and learning how to utter each letter's corresponding sounds. Patterns for how words are formed come next along with some rules in phonics. Students begin to read words, then sentences. By the end of high school, they are reading the great works and writing about what they have read. They have all the tools they need to read, write, and think in English. The process of learning the language frees them to learn endless amounts of information and to continue their learning throughout life. But the process is incremental, and it can take students more than thirteen years of consistent training to master English.

Musical training is no different. To teach music as a language, students must be saturated. Students begin learning the grammar of singing by hearing it and doing it, then gradually progress to understanding. They slowly gain all the tools they need to read, write, and think in the language of music. At the end, the process of learning music frees them to continue learning and interacting with musical compositions throughout life. This is what I call putting "musicianship between the ears."[4]

Band, orchestra, choir, strings ensemble, recorder class, and group guitar lessons are all excellent opportunities for students, but they

---

4. How many people out there are button pushers and not musicians? They were taught some techniques on a piano or violin but never developed the musicianship to hold it all together.

each bear something in common. Understood within the framework of the *Trivium*, these opportunities are rhetoric-level activities. Just as a third grader quoting Shakespeare in your school's speech meet does not indicate that he has full mastery of the English language, so a middle school string orchestra doing a lovely rendition of "Twinkle, Twinkle Little Star" does not necessarily indicate music mastery. There is an important order for ideal music training. Students need musicianship between the ears before learning the mechanics of their fingers. Forty students on a stage holding string instruments and playing might appear to indicate the needle of music literacy is pointed in the right direction. But because playing an instrument is a rhetoric-level activity, lifelong music literacy cannot be achieved without a solid foundation in the grammar of singing and musicianship. By focusing on musicianship between the ears before studying the mechanics of playing an instrument, a student can develop an aptitude for loving, appreciating, and sharing music before advancing to the polishing stage of performing in concerts and other rhetoric-level activities.

RETUNING THE SCHOOL CULTURE

James K.A. Smith, in his book *Desiring the Kingdom*, articulates a convincing case that Christians are called to view education as a "formative rather than informative project."[5] Smith explains that the right-ordered goal of education is about "forming hearts and desires" through "shaping hopes and passions."[6] In other words, to see a maturing of loves and desires in right ways, a number of things need to be purposefully woven in to the life of the school through the music culture. A school's culture of music must go deeper than just ticking off a box that tells parents the school curriculum includes music-making.

---

5. James K.A. Smith, *Desiring the Kingdom: Worship, Worldview, and Cultural Formation* (Grand Rapids: Baker Academic, 2009), 18.

6. Ibid., 18.

Joy is a great place to start. It is difficult for anyone to sing and remain sullen. Even the simple jingles of a memory lesson bring a certain energetic joy to a classroom. Truly, music-making creates a joyful fellowship wherever it goes. I find that it bears similar fruit to the effects of eating together around a table as a family. As the rooms of a *Schola cantorum* are explored, the joy of students and teachers is noticeable. This fruit of the Spirit can be cultivated in endless scenarios. Imagine the mood of a school on a big day full of tests or the mood of a school as the students who complain become louder and louder. The introduction of music to such a school would be sweet medicine. It cheers the glum and also fills the mouths of the complainers with song, slowing down their dominance during the lunch hour. All of this promotes joy on the campus. If there is singing without joy, something is amiss.

Loyalty through liturgy should also be present. As a common spirit inspires devotion within any group, so the spirit of a classical Christian school should be unifying as well. A tight group often shares a language, a way of speaking about their shared subject. See where this is going? By now, I hope you think of music as a language. **People who spend time together often will pick up on the same phrases and ways of talking. When students and faculty sing and make music together, it is no different. It will become natural for them to sing before eating. It becomes natural for them to sing at the end of the day, or sing as they tidy the lunchroom chairs, or sing as they work on the set-up for a school event. It becomes natural for them to love this liturgy and be loyal to the spirit created between them. They develop shared songs and common loves of songs that strengthen bonds and make the hard tasks of doing school and running a school much more bearable. It becomes part of the school body, fills that body and enriches it. As a student body begins to share a stockpile of songs, an *esprit de corps* follows. A *Schola cantorum* will have such a spirit.

A love of loveliness is the result of good liturgy, and this should not surprise us. The common loyalty of shared songs should develop and move into a maturing sound. With the right shepherding and careful selections, students in the school can learn to sing through a new repertoire, and the new repertoire can shape and mature their love of good music and singing. Simply listening to good music will not endear them to it in the same way. This is part of why a music appreciation class does not strike at the heart of the matter. It is the song we learn to sing that stays with us. This is an essential part of what it means to cultivate our love and train our children in the nurture and admonition (*paideia*) of the Lord.[7] We want hearts, minds, and souls of our students to love the things that are lovely. Training and discipleship are required to help them shape their loves after the ever-lovely God.

A *Schola cantorum* should also understand and teach that **singing is for service**. What do the students say about the pop musicians of the day? How do they value contemporary music acts? In a day and age where music celebrities are viewed as idols or icons, students must be reoriented to see that the musician is actually the servant, and their work and effort is a gift meant to bless others. Opportunities to teach this truth are plenteous. What I have found is that as soon as your children start to sing and make music together, it is very easy to sing for assemblies, nursing homes, church services, community gatherings and more. Short songs or canons sung tunefully by young voices have a similar effect to small drops of water on a parched tongue. In training a servant-leader culture, singing and skillful music-making is one of the best ways to serve.

Edification also occurs within the community of the classroom as making music together is a prime **tool for teaching virtue**. Placing music before students requires their submission to the notes on the

---

7. Ephesians 6:4.

page. Music sheets instruct students when to sing and when not to sing. Students are taught to work together and not exalt the self, otherwise the sound of the whole will fail. Sometimes perseverance is required to work through a difficult masterwork. From hymns to grand concerts, the culture of singing helps reinforce the lessons of self-control, self-discipline, self-sacrifice, and much more.

This part might be a bit surprising, but folk or communal dance is one of the downstream benefits of building a music culture, one that teaches **maturity in relating and maturity in pairing of music**. Schools can use the music classroom, protocol classes and balls to teach social dances. Social dances can be conducted in a group-oriented style, with longways sets and circle mixers to avoid placing two young hormonal teens in an exclusive or intimate setting during a dance. Folk dances allow us to feel the rhythm and form in music. It makes the music on a page come alive and appeals to more senses than just our hearing. The music can be *seen*, portrayed with humans moving to the music in casual and formal dances alike. The focus of folk dancing is the coordination and unity of the whole as opposed to the singular dancer. Still, individual lessons are plentiful as well. Attentive servant leadership is required by the young men in particular as they direct their partner. Everyone must learn how to properly conduct themselves with members of the opposite sex. Plus, it is just plain fun!

PRACTICAL PROGRAM BUILDING

Building or preparing a Singing School can be daunting for those just getting started. But there are plenty of ways to gain traction no matter what phase your particular school currently occupies. From the outset, I have found that a fruit from the Spirit that most affects the progress, success, and efficiency of schools pursuing music is gratefulness. Gratefulness breeds patience for when things are not moving as quickly as they could. Gratefulness keeps the ground tilled and the soil fertile for new things as they come. Gratefulness helps us to not despise the day of small beginnings when we consider just how much work always remains to be done.[8]

Take Inventory

Practically, a helpful way to start building or changing a music program is to take inventory of what strengths you already possess. What faculty, facilities, instruments, etc. do you have access to already? Maybe your part-time kindergarten aid is a musician by training and would happily make a side move to help in a new music program. It can be surprising what resources are available and untapped.

If resources are truly limited and options are not open, focus on what you can do with what you have. Be flexible and ready to hold some things loosely while other things need to be held tightly. Guiding principles and goals for music literacy, for example, need to be held tightly. Hold loosely the idea that every upper school student has to have an instrument to play. You do not have to build new buildings or have specialized classrooms or textbooks to begin. Simply put, you need to have an awareness of your families, staff, and facilities and be willing to start small.

Maintain the Language Mindset

Remember that music literacy is the goal, making language instruction the most helpful crossover pattern for teaching music. Without being overly philosophical or specially skilled in music, school administration can still work from this pattern. As with speaking, singing happens before reading and writing. Begin by having your students sing and explore how they can be more of a *Schola cantorum*. From the moment the ears are formed they begin to absorb the language around them. Similarly, songs being sung and music being played in the

---

8. Zechariah 4:10.

life of your students will prepare them for more formal instruction. Get them singing informally in chapel/convocation and throughout the life of the school. Focus on singing from the earliest ages possible.

Big Space vs. Mobile Classroom

An active music class is best facilitated in an open, larger space where students can move and sing. The younger classes can sit on the floor in a circle and move with the teacher's instruction to feel the beat and make music in a circular group. This music can spring forth into song activities or dances that create a joyful learning atmosphere disguised as play and fun. The bigger the space, the more options for the teacher to adapt the instruction to the age and ability of the group in front of them.

The alternative "mobile" classroom (by that I mean a teacher who walks from classroom to classroom) has to rework some of these things to bring about active music-making, but it can be done. Maybe the desks are quickly moved to the perimeter of the classroom when the teacher arrives. Maybe the games or song activities are modified to be conducive to a smaller space. If your school has extra wide hallways, even this could be a temporary option. The teacher will probably need a large rolling cart to transport teaching tools and, if possible, some centrally located shelves in the facility if they do not have a designated classroom. These are simple temporary adaptations for a mobile classroom style.

For me personally, I used to have a wide open classroom measuring about forty square feet. Our school is in a new location now, and I teach in a space that is basically a small-box theater. The only space to move is between the stage and the first row of seating. This has proved to be a challenge and has caused me to tweak and re-work games and activities accordingly. Teachers are resilient and can make creative modifications. Go ahead and start, even without the ideal space.

The Teacher is the Curriculum

The biggest curricular decision you will make as a Singing School is who you hire to do the job of teaching music. Students will forget the textbook they used in their favorite class in high school before they forget the name of their favorite teacher. The skilled teacher in the music literacy-driven classroom is able to model a love of the subject as well as a proficiency above the level of the students. The skilled music teacher is able to guide the students to discovery of the material being presented rather than just unwrapping it for them in the form of a lecture. It is not mandatory that a Singing School teacher have raw musical talent, but because the Lord has given voices to all our students, teachers who know how to develop those young voices is ideal. If your resources include a professional percussionist who is not able to sing and a lady with a music degree who sang in choirs her whole life, the lady might be the better option for your young program. The music teacher will need some level of expertise but does not have to be perfect in every way. Douglas Wilson describes the best kind of teaching as,

> loving the subject matter in the presence of students whom you love, which can only be done if you are doing this *Coram Deo*, 'in the presence of God.' So, if you are loving God by loving the material in a classroom full of students that you love, that love is contagious. Love bestows loveliness. As you love in this way, the students start to get worked up and excited in the same way because we learn, the Bible teaches, by imitation. It says in Ephesians 5:1, 'Therefore, dearly loved children, be imitators of God.' We learn by imitation. We are called to learn

by imitation. And so the children are supposed to be imitating you.[9]

There is no other way around it. The teacher will be imitated by the students. This is particularly crucial in the subject of music. The one teaching must be able to both carry a tune and set the tone for your program. As the Lord blesses and we are faithful to continue to train our students, the bar for a music teacher can always be raised as new resources become available.

A Flexible Schedule

Where music classes meet and how many times your music teacher instructs the students will likely require flexibility during a Singing School's early stages. Simply keep advancing, orienting the music training and schedules around giving students proficiency and mastery. The importance of saturation cannot be emphasized enough. Students immersed in a foreign language will have better success than those who are simply reading and hearing words in a different language. Gear the schedule towards that end.

For example, if you are able to see your students once a week for an hour, gives thanks and make it work as best you can. Then sit down with your school leadership and ask whether that hour-long session could be split it into two 30-minute meeting times. Try that for a while, then ask for 20-minute lessons that happen on three different days in the week. The benefit of lessening time between meetings is that the material and repetition are fresh for the students. This is the way our scheduling should trend in language-type instruction. If music is going to be taught in a history or music appreciation or fine arts model, it really does not matter if you take a semester off or have one class per week during the single semester per year. But if you are going to prepare

---

9. Douglas Wilson, "Personal Holiness" Lecture, *2004 Repairing the Ruins ACCS National Conference*, Atlanta, GA, June 24, 2004.

students to read, hear, sing, and enjoy music-making, then they need as much immersion and repetition as possible. Gradually refine your schedule to a more conducive environment for language immersion of music.

Earnest Leadership

A school's board of directors has the means and the incentive to be out front in communicating to the parents the importance of music literacy instruction in the life of the students. The challenge is connecting a Singing School's vision to the practical concerns needed to bring about that vision. A good head of school has likely read the classics and the church fathers on the importance of music, but that same headmaster is juggling so many other duties that he may not know what resources a music teacher needs or is using. Ideally, a board member with some musical training could assist in such a situation.

The best resources for school boards in overcoming the challenges of juggling decisions over music choices is to keep the school leaders in proximity to other schools which are doing similar things. Whether that is attending conferences, participating in music workshops, visiting other music programs, or otherwise, imitation and community will be some of the best encouragement and help to boards who are trying to navigate the area of music education.

HOW TO START TODAY

Maybe you are reading this book, and it is the end of summer. The teachers for your school are already hired, the schedule is settled. There is no room this year for a music program. Maybe your school is brand new, with only a handful of students and even fewer teachers, stretched to the max, each covering a multitude of subjects. Yet you are convinced that a new music program or a more robust music program must be initiated. There are a number of things your school can start right away, even mid-year, and all of them are budget friendly.

Pick a School Song, Hymn, or Anthem

Choose one that can galvanize the student body and encapsulate what it is that you do as a school. Maybe your school picks the famous Latin hymn, "Non nobis domine," a three-part canon set to music by William Byrd. This particular hymn can be a great selection as a school anthem. Is there already a school hymn or alma mater, but none of the students have learned it? Pull it out! Perhaps over time, you could have one commissioned (but that is not a requirement, of course). At my school we have chosen "Rise Again, Ye Lion-hearted" as our school anthem with its "Grant that I may ever be loyal, staunch, and true to Thee."[10] These songs help provide traditions that strengthen that *esprit de corps* mentioned earlier. The songs chosen do not have to be easy enough for everyone to read and learn on their own. It is perfectly fine to practice learning a song that challenges the students. Just have the youngest singers memorize and learn by rote from their teachers or a recording. Any time the school body gathers as a whole, make your school song a regular part of the tradition, especially for events that include parents. Place a copy of the school song at the end of a school program and invite the attendees to join in with the students as they conclude the program with the school song.

Sing at Assemblies and Lunch Gatherings

A quick place to jumpstart this singing approach is at any assembly or gathering of students and faculty. Morning convocation, snack time, lunch time, end of the day, and so on. Pick a rotation of short hymns,

---

10. *The Lutheran Hymnal* (St. Louis: Concordia Publishing House, 1941), 470. The ending line of the fourth verse.

songs or prayers that the whole school can learn. This will be good preparation for formal music classes if you are unable to immediately formalize a music program. Kent Young's "Singing in the Cracks" has practical ideas on this concept. Communicating the importance of singing regularly and releasing the pressure of feeling like it has to be a grand performance are both fruits from this more casual music-making. The students become comfortable with the social and communal aspects of it.

THE GLORIOUS DAY OF SMALL BEGINNINGS

It is too easy to be discouraged when first starting any large task. It would be better to have students exposed to lots of singing and no classes than nothing at all. When we hold tightly to the language learning metaphor, we are reminded that we are learning way before we ever hear a formal lesson presented in a class. In the same way, your students are on the path to music literacy simply by having your school sing and prioritize the doing of music and not just the hearing of it. If resources are limited, and you are only able to have limited music instruction and singing work, start with the lowest grades and build up from there. Keep adding another year to the music training schedule, and before long, those kindergarteners will be graduating high school, pulling behind them a thirteen-year music literacy program! Give thanks where you are and ask the Lord's blessings on continued patient growth in this area as you do in the other areas of school life and work.

5

JOYFUL MUSIC LITERACY

How to Teach Music Classically

JARROD RICHEY

The Kodály approach is the most well-suited music education philosophy for the classical Christian school paradigm if we want our students to be fully literate in the language of music. Without thinking through a philosophy of music education properly, it is easy for schools to settle on something familiar or be satisfied as long as music is being covered in their curriculum somehow. This will not suffice. Skipping the details in the area of music training will only yield stunted fruit like that of many secular schools, a pitiful substitute for the monuments to which we aspire. It will be hard work, but it must be done. G.K. Chesterton once famously compared an open mouth to an open mind, the object of each being to close on something.[1] Classical Christian schools need to close on a good strategy for educating their

---

1. Gilbert Keith Chesterton, *Illustrated London News*, October 10, 1908. "Merely having an open mind is nothing. The object of opening

pupils in music. The temptation in many classical Christian schools is simply to allow the teacher to pick whichever music education philosophy best suits their personality and preference. Leaving all the decisions to that year's teacher is not a strategy, it is dodging the duty of thoughtfulness in all areas of education. The challenge for classical Christian schools is to latch on to the approach which matches both the Christian worldview as well as the way that students are best taught.

INTRODUCTION TO KODÁLY

Zoltán Kodály a late nineteenth and early twentieth century composer who lived in communist Hungary, believed all children could be taught music literacy. He maintained that a culture's native songs, as learned from birth, would be the most helpful catalog of music for students' instruction and that only the best song material would be suitable (a parallel with the type of literature we choose in classical schools to teach English literacy).[2] The method that developed under his guidance in Hungary changed musical literacy standards and consequently the culture in Hungary. Even today there are numerous major orchestras, opera companies, and other professional ensembles

---

the mind, as of opening the mouth, is to shut it again on something solid." Similarly, in another article he stated, "Mouths and minds were made to shut; they were made to open only in order to shut."

2. Zoltán Kodály, *The Selected Writings of Zoltan Kodály* (London; New York: Boosey & Hawkes, 1974), 122. "Let us stop the teachers' superstition according to which only some diluted art-substitute is suitable for teaching purposes. A child is the most susceptible and the most enthusiastic audience for pure art; for in every great artist the child is alive—and this is something felt by youth's congenial spirit. Conversely, only art of intrinsic value is suitable for children! Everything else is harmful. After all, food is more carefully chosen for an infant than for an adult. Musical nourishment which is 'rich in vitamins' is essential for children."

that can be attributed to the work of Kodály and others who shared his vision of music for all.[3] The high-yielding work of music literacy spread to America in the 1960s and picked up serious momentum in the 1970s as American music pedagogues modified and adapted the approach in the United States.[4]

The Kodály (pronounced CODE-eye) philosophy of music education easily aligns with the stages of the classical model of teaching. Specifically, the language-based approach for instruction means that in the early years there is a grammar-like approach to singing and making music. Initial teaching of 50-100 songs by hearing, rote, and reading provides the known material that can be sequentially unearthed and contextualized for the student based on learning ability and age. This leads to a mastery in literacy—the ability to read music, analyze music and compose original musical offerings. Additionally, the human singing voice is given primary focus in the Kodály approach as opposed to using instruments for primary instruction. The emphasis on the voice first gives students a tool for a lifetime of learning music which dovetails nicely with the classical pedagogy. Kodály stated, "Teach music and singing at school in such a way that it is not a torture but a joy for the pupil; instill a thirst for finer music in him, a thirst which will last for a lifetime."[5] He believed the best way to unlock that lifetime of music was through singing.[6]

---

3. Ibid., 199. "Real art is one of the most powerful forces in the rise of mankind, and he who renders it accessible to as many people as possible is a benefactor of humanity."

4. Kodály's philosophy came to the U.S. through the work of folks like Katinka Scipiades Dániel, Denis Bacon, Lois Choksy, Sister Lorna Zemke, and subsequent others.

5. Kodály, *The Selected Writings*, 120.

6. Ibid., 206. "If one were to attempt to express the essence of this education in one word, it could only be—singing."

It is a common misunderstanding that the Kodály philosophy (or approach) of music education simply refers to using solfege syllables and the hand signs to match. But the Guidonian syllables and the John Curwen Hand Signs both pre-date Kodály. Instead these tools (among others) are used by Kodály teachers to help ground their music instruction in a language-based model.[7] Sound and rhythm are taught by active participation in singing and making music, followed by learning to phoneticize them through the use of solfege. This is only a small step in the training process. The Kodály pedagogy is actually a full system of how to sequentially teach students from the early years until they reach proficiency in music years later.

A Walk into the Kodály Music Classroom

The Kodály classroom is a singing classroom. An observer in the room will notice right away that singing is a part of almost every activity. Whether singing games, canons, rounds, or improvised melodies, the classroom is filled with the voices of the students. Even quiet moments of the room are used for musical thinking and inner hearing so the students may hear in their head first what they must sing second.

The Kodály classroom is not a parrot cage where little birds learn to speak back exactly what is spoken to them. Instead, the teacher is the model who can help guide the students through new sounds, rhythms, and musical experiences by doing (then learning about the full meaning later). The classroom is a full-body experience. The kinds of activities are varied in the day-to-day classroom. Students will be sitting one

---

7. "The Guidonian hand" is a mnemonic tool used in the Middle Ages by a monk, Guido of Arezzo, to help in teaching sight-reading. Later, nineteenth century English minister John Curwen's hand signs were developed to help church members learn to read music with skill. It's important to know that in both cases, these tools pre-date Kodály even though they are merely tools that are visible at a glance to help people recognize Kodály's approach to music education.

minute and the next minute moving or dancing to the song material they were just rehearsing or reviewing. They are sitting on the floor clapping out a rhythm or standing at a board filling in the solfege sounds for what the instructor sang as they entered the classroom. There might be a role-play song or a call and response song, even a folk partner dance. The Kodály classroom is active, not passive. The activities establish the songs in the students' bodies and minds, while also endearing them to it. They are not simply told *about* music.

TRIVIUM APPLIED: THE EARLY YEARS

The grammar stage of music instruction is the time when the students' minds are like sponges. They need to hear and do as much as possible. Children first hear and say hundreds of words before they know the meaning of each word. They use words in sentences after hearing them spoken around them. They do not know what part of speech the words belong to, nor do they possess a complete definition for each word. But the learning is there. It is merely below the surface. That is the model of language learning, and that is the beauty of the Kodály philosophy.

In the classical model of music education the grammar of music should first focus on the human singing voice, the first step in literacy. The emphasis on voice first as well as inner hearing ensures that musicianship is pursued in the training process. There is no need to jump to rhetoric-level activities which place an excessive burden on the motor skills of our earliest budding musicians. Fill them with song in their grammar years. Teach them how to sing and explore their own singing abilities. All the musical stories, patterns, songs, rounds, and games they learn become a repository for later lessons in their music training as well.

Learning is mostly disguised as play in the early stages of Kodály music instruction. Students sing and match pitch through song games and activities. Disguising the assessment of the students' abilities and progress through these games is effective as well as fun for them. Echo songs and pitch exploration activities like making siren sounds stretch the students in use of their voices. Having students tap and feel the beat of a song helps lay the foundation for music's patterns of sounds in meter. Without being too technical, this process is one big varied game of "same/different." Students are being trained in the differences between high and low, soft and loud, big and little, fast and slow, short and long, and so forth. They touch their heads if they hear a high sound, and they touch their shoulders if they hear a slightly lower sound. They are physically, aurally, and visually gathering ways to refine their ability to hear, do, and discern.

Memorization of musical terms and facts at this stage needs to be done minimally. Too often, music terms are given to children when the words are not grounded properly to other known material. The ideas become abstract bits of information instead of concrete facts connected in a logical order. Kodály training would have those facts of music be presented in a sequential system that brings the student along slowly to greater awareness of music.

Visual comparatives of big and little begin basic reading of music in lower grades. As students learn a song like "Rain, Rain, Go Away" they can touch pictures of an umbrella on a chart or on a paper to help them engage in the tactile practice of reading a steady heart beat, one umbrella per beat. They do not need to know that they are "reading rhythm" (an abstract concept) because the teacher is simply preparing them for that concept later. Move to preparing rhythm with those same icons in different sizes to show quarter and eighth notes respectively. Simplified stick notation (still without relation to the staff or clef) can be introduced next followed by the difference of two notes of high/low on two lines.

Reading music can start as reading icons on a simplified staff. Slowly introduce a limited range of sounds for them to read. Solfege syllables are great for this. Give only two lines to begin staff introduction, then three, etc., sequentially bringing them to reading music in solfege sounds on the five-line staff like we sequentially bring them to reading words. The benefit of this process is that we are not just dumping facts on them but helping them to slowly advance their learning without frustration. As adults, we struggle to think like children when it comes to how to present music material. We project on their little frames the idea that knowing the names and definitions will help them be able to progress in music understanding. In reality, it is putting a logic/dialectic activity ahead of a grammar activity. Claiming proudly that "my first grade music students can name all the lines on the treble clef" or "my students know the four families of the orchestra" is merely a mirage of literacy success.

All of this is summarized under the idea of hearing and doing.[8] That is the grammar stage pattern of music training for the classical music classroom. Good modeling of singing and voice exploration for the student is the focus. Students are soaking up a world of singing, and they are being prepared for guided discovery for years to come.

First Grade Classroom Example

To get a better idea of what a classical Christian school music class with a Kodály emphasis actually looks like, let us walk through a

---

8. "Doing" music can be ambiguous, but it is the best word I have found that can cover the various active parts of music-making like singing, moving, dancing, etc.

sample class for first graders. In the first grade classroom with music classes held two to three times each week for 20-30 minutes, the pace of the lesson and the efficiency of the lesson are paramount, filling every minute for a burst of immersive language style instruction.

Whether the teacher goes to the students, or the students come to the teacher, the lesson immediately begins with a sung greeting such as: "Good morning, singers," followed by, "Good morning, Mr. Richey." The greeting provides exploration of voice ranges, tuning of ear, and focusing of mind. This greeting can be as simple as one note or several notes complimenting the range and stage of the class. The teacher may briefly tell the story of a farmer or animal to weave the day's song games and activities together smoothly, then take the front student's hand to lead them all into a circle formation. Students begin to sing and enact the game of "The Farmer in the Dell" song, and the teacher mentions that the cat in the song was very mischievous transitioning them all to singing the song, "Naughty Kitty Cat." These songs have several music concepts being planted and watered through repetition and familiarity over time. From there the teacher might go to a review activity of patting heart beats to a known song or tapping rhythm sticks to identify a song written out in simplified stick notation. Students take turns. They may be able to listen to a song rhythm and see if they can assemble the rhythm with popsicle sticks or with pencil and paper on a worksheet.

The combinations are numerous, and the flow is left to the creativity of the teacher. There is very little instruction like, "Now class, I would like you to . . ." or "Class, would you like to . . .?" Instead the first grade Kodály music teacher is moving seamlessly from one thing to the next, hardly saying an uninstructive word, constantly challenging and stretching their little brains. The teacher might remind the students about the farmer's son named John who went to sleep and didn't wake up early enough the next morning until his siblings came in and sang, "Are you sleeping, Brother John?" to him. Your students will jump right in and sing. They eventually will have the confidence to sing it in rounds together. Then the teacher sings goodbye to the students individually or to the whole class as they line up to dismiss. This scenario may seem silly, but remember that after adults go to college they tend to bring back the last bit of teaching they received.[9] Students love the childlikeness of it, and the lesson goes by in a flash. Management and discipline troubles are joyfully choked out if the lesson is planned and executed well by the teacher.

Don't Rush to the Music Staff

In the first year or two of training, the full music staff is barely needed. Students are taught to read intervals using solfege sounds rather than note or absolute letter names (A, B, C, etc.) on the staff. Teachers often rush to give the youngest of budding musicians a full staff and teach them the letter names on the treble and bass clef. But if this is not connected to concrete understanding it can be more frustrating than helpful in the early years of learning music. For many teachers this is the hardest hurdle when considering the Kodály approach to music literacy.

From introduction to the staff, gradually move students to be able to read on numerous clefs by teaching them to sound out what they see. We want them to see and hear music "in the same way that an educated

---

9. Tom Garfield, founding administrator for Logos School in Moscow, ID and one of the pioneers of the ACCS has said numerous times over years at conferences, "Teachers teach as they have been taught, until taught otherwise." The last bit of teaching that music teachers likely received was by an adult instructing adults how to teach. The disconnect between likes and abilities of adults and children causes the adult to not want to be "childish." The first time you apply some of these things, the faces of your youngest singers will light up, and you will too.

adult will read a book: in silence, but imagining the sound."[10] This skill is called "inner hearing" or sometimes "audiation."[11] The student has to hear the sound in their head much like one can hear the sound of a word when they read it silently to themselves. There are resources and games that help this activity take place. But the general idea is that the reading of music and rhythm be a mental activity.

Fourth Grade Classroom Example

By the time the students are in fourth grade they have been singing together for several years. They know about 75-100 songs, and they also know a lot of things about these songs—some that have been taught by the teacher and some that they have discovered on their own. They should know the pentatonic scale of music, and they are months away from learning the rest of the solfege sounds that make up the major scale.[12] They can sing songs in rounds and canons tunefully. The classroom flow is similar to the younger grades, but with more individual opportunities to sing and demonstrate mystery songs for one another. Students also have more tools by now and need less narrative

---

10. Kodály, *The Selected Writings*, 204.

11. "Audiation" is a term first coined by music educator Edwin Gordon in 1975. The term describes the practice of hearing and thinking of music material internally, sometimes called inner-hearing by others in the Kodály and broader music education field. Gordon's use of audiation has a more specific and prescribed practice than the general use I am giving it here to refer to the notion of internalizing music.

12. The pentatonic scale of music consists of the five-scale degrees that are whole steps apart as opposed to half steps. *do, re, mi, so, la* without having *fa* or *ti* present because they are harder to tune in younger years. Or if solfege syllables are unfamiliar then maybe C,D,E,G,A are easier illustrations where F is omitted because E-F is a half step and B-C is also a half step.

to bond the lesson together. The ending of one song can be repeated in an ostinato by the students, and the teacher can start singing the next song in the lesson, making interesting music together.

    A sung greeting begins the lesson. That sung greeting will be more complex and varied in sound and rhythm based on the level of the older class. Longer story songs may be there but less overt as in the younger classes. A mystery song shown from the teacher's silent hand signs or pre-written notation on the dry erase board may be the jumping-off point for that particular lesson. A student can step in front of the class and silently hand sign a known song to the class and see if the class can sing it in their head and recognize it. The teacher helps the students with part-work and improvising of scenarios and rhymes in songs. The students can sing the words to songs and hand sign the solfege at the same time. They will be able to hear a rhythm and wait two beats and clap behind the teacher or the student modeling for them. They can read solfege on the staff and they know the absolute letter names on the staff (after several years of practicing first reading on a solfege "do" clef where they learn the relationship of solfege letters to the lines and spaces and how they can move with the various key changes). They've learned about 8th and 16th notes as well as syncopated 8ths and quarters. They can explore, and they are eager to be shown new things. The ways to stretch them in greetings and canons are vast. They are getting close to being able to read most basic music put in front of them. If they can't read it easily they are able to do enough to figure it out similarly to a 5th or 6th grader being able to clunkily sound out a difficult word even if they are not sure of the meaning. From here the fifth and sixth grades would do further singing and studying to finish off the sequence of Kodály instructions that should leave them equipped to read music for themselves.

TRIVIUM APPLIED: THE MIDDLE SCHOOL YEARS

The logic/dialectic stage is the time when students minds graduate from assimilating facts through memorization to categorizing and questioning the hierarchy of previously learned concepts. They begin to ask why. They are ready to visually decipher or decode same and different in more complex ways. The dialectic and logic stage of music development can be reached about the same time as other classroom activities provided that the students are getting regular enough music instruction to match their age progression. If not, then the teacher can watch for when they are starting to ask and pull apart the different parts of the song material they have learned as an indicator of their readiness.

This stage is full of students being able to pick up on patterns and wondering what is coming next in the sequence of learning. Ideally, in the school's singing and music culture the students are noticing the more advanced things they see written on song sheets and that they hear done by older classes and choir groups. A school's mature musical culture makes the logic students yearn to advance to the next step, further discovery of new material, but also more expanded singing and music-making. They can sing songs while tapping rhythms. By four or five years of instruction, they have a working knowledge of music-making. They also might be able to sing and make harmonies with their ear but not know how to categorize those harmonies or why they should. This discovery comes as the teacher helps them connect the dots already put in place. The students move from "sound to symbol" where they learn more by hearing and doing in the grammar years, to increasingly being able to do from sight.[13] They can read and count and

---

13. T.H. Yorke Trotter, *The Making of Musicians: The Rhythmic Method of Teaching Music* (London: Herbert Jenkins Ltd, 1914), 76. Trotter wrote that a child "must first have the effect in his mind before he knows the symbols that should be used to express that effect." He

decode music. They can see things and make connections themselves. They will wonder why this is connected to that. They will wonder why do we do this and not that in a particular song. Teachers have all those inquisitive opportunities in every direction—singing, reading, and writing of music.

The logic stage of development is where singing and performance can really start to pick up, for the area of music study lends itself to performance much more naturally than math formulas and history facts. The songs being used to decode and learn become a great way for students to perform for those around them. Their performances correspond nicely to formal logic training because they are able to make yet another connection between what they deliver and how they deliver it when they sing and perform for others. Once again, this is not a hard and fast stage that is always tied closely to a particular age or precise grade. If your students have had music instruction two or three times a week since they began school then you might see a 5th and 6th grade group beginning to stretch their wings in logic and dialectic abilities and inquisitiveness. If students are only being instructed in choir that is performance-driven or they only have music once a week or every few weeks then this logic stage of music making might not happen before high school. Just watch for their readiness to progress.

---

states that notation "should come after, and not before, the feeling for music has been developed." This understanding was adopted by hymn composer and music educator Lowell Mason in New England, and carried on to ideas by Shinichi Suzuki and others. This is not new to Kodály philosophy but Kodály philosophy is firmly rooted in the notion of sound experience before symbol experience. Swiss educator Heinrich Pestalozzi (1746-1827) is believed to be the first recorded source of the "sound to symbol" principle of learning.

TRIVIUM APPLIED: THE LATTER YEARS

This stage of learning is the creative and culminating stage in music. It is, of course, the performance and delivery in choir, band, orchestra, or other performance opportunities of the material gleaned and learned into a winsome presentation. But beyond that, the rhetoric stage should include the ability to create and design within the craft of music. Copying the works of great composers is the final task before students begin to create and design music. Writing short pieces of music and compositions is the goal, just like writing of poems and short stories are the rhetoric-level activities in English and literature classes.

The classical methodology is steeped in the liberal arts tradition valuing the benefit to studying beyond the simple, practical day-to-day activities. So whether or not our students seek to be English teachers we teach them the grammar, history, and composition of our language. In a similar way our students should be able to create and compose musical ideas and works, whether or not they become musicians by trade. They must know the system of music notation. In generations past when digital copying and digitized scoring was not available, students had to hand-copy the score(s) needed for the upcoming piece or work. This apprenticeship allowed for pupils to quite literally duplicate the masters' works and scan the works into their minds. This is rarely done anymore. The study of music is no longer a common feature of education, and so it is not a surprise that people cannot excel in the rudimentary disciplines of singing and reading music. By extension it becomes hard to focus on what the needs of writing music should be today. Simply put, students should be taught to take down the music and rhythms they hear played or sung for them. Once again, as with reading instruction, music reading and dictation does not have to happen all at once. Students can work in rhythms only for a time. They can also focus on the sounds they hear. This music dictation will likely lag somewhat behind their ability to sing and to read. But this area of training in music literacy is important just the same.

For this reason, it is beneficial for students to practice sight-reading and music dictation and copying for years, though this is not mandatory. Throughout the stages of their music literacy training, they will likely be writing down first stick rhythms and solfege, and then rhythms and melodies on the staff. You might even have them compose music melodies of a few beats using tight parameters. It is not as if they only begin to compose when they are musical 11th and 12th graders. Hopefully, they have been experimenting in your classroom all along the way. In my classroom, there have been guided composition of hymn texts to a tune composed by the students. Other more advanced classes have composed melodies and then harmonized them into four parts like what a hymn writer would do. Classes taught by highly proficient instructors might teach their students formal species counterpoint and even some J.S. Bach part-writing practice and analysis. But the students' work does not have to be high art composition. I have had classes take a text from scripture and make a canon or round from it in class. In their writing and arranging of music, they develop an appreciation for music unlike the effect of peering in on the work of others. Have the students write a canon and struggle with that. Then play for them crab canons by Bach that work forward, backward and inverted, and they will have a newfound appreciation for such skill. The possibilities are truly endless, the most helpful advice that I can give being use wisdom as the instructor who knows the frame and aptitude of the class.

Rhetoric Music Classroom Example

Ideally, by the rhetoric stage, the students' music class time should be a mixture of rhetoric-level activities and singing of a great catalog of music. Classes should explore canons and literature by singing and doing then decoding based on the concepts known to the students. Students should have awareness of styles of music, having sampled a good many styles from the ancient era to the modern period. They should have the ability to sing and understand the church modes in early compositions. They can work on harmonizing in small bits and in explaining key signatures and larger patterns in works. Their ability to analyze the formal structure of music and hear works in class is greatly improved. They can pick up and read a piece of music at least part of the way through before hearing any of it played for them.

The rhetoric class' activities depend on several things. Has this class had music training throughout each year since the early grades? Has there been significant turnover of students and new student transfers who are changing the level of the class? If this is the case in your classroom and you are still stuck with those students who have transferred in and are playing catch up on solfege and counting and the various language aspects of music, then sing, sing, sing. Sing great works where you extract doable parts. Help them with what solfege sounds to sing. Give them canons and rounds both old and new that don't even have words attached to them and let them joyfully work through the growing pains of catching up. You will leave them happier and more skilled.

If a class has been training in music since kindergarten, what might a senior class be capable of in the ideal scenario? This is the class that is able to sing and perform new material in class, discuss some of the connective parts and context for the music that is sung, and also write down melodies being played or sung for them. This group should have experience at composing a melody on a given text, harmonizing that same text so that a choir of sopranos, altos, tenors, and basses could sing it together. They will have sung as a choir at various points. Their class will have begun to function as a choir and the possibility to perform those pieces that were just sight-reading exercises could quickly become workable into school assembly performances or events.

This group should know enough about keys to see a hymn and be able to tell what key it is in. They should be able to look at a symphony score and see where the piece shifts to the dominant key. They should be able to hear and work through the complex forms present in the style of writing known as counterpoint. They should be led into these exercises not to stir up pride, but so that they know what has come before them and can refine and pass it on to those who come after them. The seniors will have an education that prepares them to be active worshipping Christians who are able to participate in music-making all their days. If our work for them is done well, they will be fully literate in the language of music. Skillful, joyful music making is the goal; choir and instrumental performance are the measurable fruits of this.

HAVING MULTIPLE SUBJECTS

One of the ways to expand our programs entails dividing instruction into multiple subjects. I realize that when trying to persuade administrators of the need for music time, it is very unlikely to get more than music classes and maybe choir/instrumental ensembles at first. But if a school has separate times of instruction in the phonics of English and the history of English literature, then there may be times of value in having multiple areas of music instruction under the large umbrella of music literacy. A school could schedule their performing ensembles as an extra-curricular activity while scheduling music classes as part of the normal school day. I am not necessarily advocating for different period classes for music history, theory, choir, composition, etc. Rather, my point is to highlight the notion that if we are going to teach music as a language we need to provide music instruction through layered areas of learning. These areas can fall under one "musical omnibus" class that is referred to as musicianship class. Such a class could have components of singing, sight-reading, writing, dictation, history, and active listening. Simply having a choir or catch-all music class is not enough. We would do well to rethink and stretch our understanding of how best to categorize music training in our schools, not allowing it to be an afterthought or the last thing we think to prioritize in the school schedule. "We must pray for wisdom," says Joshua Drake, "so that our musical studies will not become something that we neutrally insert 'for your glory' at the end."[14]

WHEN STUDENTS START INSTRUMENTS

Following the blossoming of students' voices after several years of singing and musicianship training, they will be more ready to study other instruments.[15] The old adage is that we want musicians, not button-pushers. We want students who are musical in and out and not just able to decode a treble and bass clef in such a way that allows them to consequently push the series of notes on a piano or similar instrument. The mechanics of an instrument can be learned easily when the musicianship and inner understanding of music making is present in the student. Classical pedagogy fully applied should see the benchmark for needing instruments when students possess the ability to sing and read with their voice before they struggle with the fingerings and intonation of a stringed instrument like a violin or cello. As Kodály said, "To teach a child an instrument without first giving him preparatory training and without developing singing, reading and dictating to the highest level along with the playing is to build upon sand."[16] Musicianship needs to be cultivated separately first, without bringing too quickly the distraction of the mechanics of instrument.

---

14. Joshua F. Drake, *Recovering Music Education as a Christian Liberal Art* (Mountain Home, AR: Borderstone Press, 2010), 121.

15. This blossoming should not be regarded as prescriptive of an exact age, but descriptive of ability and musical readiness.

16. Kodály, *The Selected Writings*, 196.

Instead of merely searching for the spot to place a finger, a musically literate student knows from inner hearing the sound he is trying to make.

KODÁLY TEACHER TRAINING

One of the advantages to the Kodály method is that an already proficient music teacher can easily learn the tools of Kodály for use in their classroom. It would be quite discouraging to suggest that they pivot to a robust music literacy focus without a ready way to help reorient and strengthen the teachers who will be doing this most important work. If your choir, band, or general music teacher can get their Kodály certification, you will see the payouts right away in your program.

Typically, Kodály Music teacher certification is awarded after completing three to four courses that last two or three weeks each summer. There are 20-30 programs across the country that provide national training and certification in this philosophy. New Saint Andrews College has one of the newest training programs, and it is geared specifically for ACCS and Christian school teachers in its Chenaniah Summer Music Institute held each summer. The training is two-fold in its focus. First teachers are instructed and coached in their own personal musicianship through singing, conducting, and solfege to be further equipped as skillful music teachers. Secondly, the teacher is taught through modeling both the Kodály sequence and methodology of how to bring students to music literacy. Each summer course in the certification is referred to by a level number (Level 1, Level 2, and Level 3). Each of these levels has a focus and theme and culminates with the teacher being given many new tools and methods to teach music literacy effectively. During the training course, teachers sing in a choir; take special topics courses on folk dancing, improvisation, music of the Bible; and research examples helpful to training the specific song concepts in the Kodály sequence. The courses are ideal for training a music teacher to lead classrooms into full music literacy instead of simply providing a fine arts survey or music appreciation course. I like to say that this summer course training is the most exhaustingly good time you will have as a music teacher. Upon successful completion of Level 3, the teacher would be considered a certified Kodály music teacher. This endorsed certification is held by the Organization of American Kodály Educators (OAKE).[17]

The Kodály philosophy is not perfect, but it does provide a specialized sequence and template for teachers to flesh out and develop into a curriculum of their own. Teachers can be trained by other teachers on how to teach sequentially and how to strengthen their own musicianship so that they can be the best teacher possible for their students. If you desire a music literacy approach but you feel overwhelmed at the lack of budget for instruments, curriculum, etc, then look at the Kodály philosophy. It is the best complement and alignment that I have seen for the classical Christian pedagogy to date. It best fleshes out those practices and emphases that make good sequential instruction in the classroom.

METHODS BEYOND KODÁLY

While the pedagogical recommendations of this book are focused on the Kodály philosophy of music instruction, that should not be taken as a total rejection of the other methods of music education available to the skilled and advanced music instructor. Orff-Schulwerk and Suzuki methods, for example, are similar to the Kodály approach in that they are "sound to symbol"-focused and literacy-focused. The chief distinction of these methods to Kodály is that they both require instruments and as discussed elsewhere in this book, the most fundamental fruit and goal

---

17. The website of the Organization of American Kodály Educators (OAKE) is www.oake.org and has a listing of officially endorsed Kodály summer programs from across the country.

in music literacy is first musicianship through singing before growing into instrumentation and other mature forms of music making. Singing is the gateway to music literacy. From there the playing of instruments is a welcome rhetoric-level activity.[18] The apparent success of having an orchestra perform on stage does not mean that the performers possess literacy and musicianship between the ears. They may be quite technically savvy at the mechanics of playing but have not been trained beyond that. Student ensemble performance could be misdiagnosed as a mark of music literacy by virtue of the fact that performance is confused with internal ability to read, write, and sing.

If performances are held up as the goal, then poor concessions will be made in the instruction and pedagogy of music. The litmus test of this for the teacher or school administrator is questions like these, "Were the students taught by rote more than by reading it themselves? Could they read and play through the music on their own leaving the bulk of the instructor's work in the area of artistry, blend, technique, etc.?" If students are taught by rote and drilled their notes for the concert but cannot read them, there is not a balance of their musicianship and performance abilities. It is nice to give students performance opportunities along the way, even those that are beyond their current understanding of music. But do too much of this and you will find that you may pull off some moving concerts but the students will not be able to continue to make music without relying on crutches. How many out there can claim a version of this very thing in their private piano or instrument lessons? How many people have taken lessons for years but walked away from them without the ability to keep going and enjoy the fruits of that instruction? There may be many reasons for that. But

---

18. By "rhetoric level activity" I am referring more to music ability and not so much a specific grade such as the tenth or eleventh grades.

more than likely, the students failed to grasp musicianship and were taught instead to orient themselves around button pushing, or the mere mechanics of performing.

So, with the right focus, the tools and facets of other methodologies can be successfully woven into the classroom as desired by the skilled teacher. Many students have benefitted from combining some of the best parts of more than one approach. A book like this can only give so much attention to all the methodologies that are available. And since other methodology tools fit well into the Kodály methodology, not the reverse, it makes a good foundation.

CONCLUSION

Kodály's approach should be that of our association of music teachers. In 1954 he summarized what a good musician should have:

> (1) a well-trained ear, (2) a well-trained intelligence, (3) a well-trained heart, (4) a well-trained hand. All four must develop together, in constant equilibrium. As soon as one lags behind or rushes ahead, there is something wrong. So far most of you have met only the requirement of the fourth point: the training of your fingers has left the rest far behind. You would have achieved the same results more quickly and easily, however, if your training in the other three had kept pace.[19]

As the ACCS and Christian schools revive the important work of music education in the training of our students, we should again heed the words of Zoltán Kodály who noted that his own native Hungary

---

19. Kodály, *The Selected Writings*, 197.

did what we are no less tempted to do—"put up the fancy spires first."[20] We need to lay a foundation of singing and training from the earliest years and not build the spires without foundation to anchor it and walls below to support it. May God grant us thankfulness of heart and clarity of purpose in our pursuit to glorify him in the training of our young musicians.

---

20. Ibid., 127. "We put up the fancy spires first. When we saw that the whole edifice was shaky, we set to building the walls. We have still to make a cellar. This has been the situation, particularly in our musical culture. If in 1875 instead of establishing the Academy of Music, we had laid the foundations for the teaching of singing in schools, today's musical culture would be greater and more general."

6

WISDOM IN MUSIC PROGRAM BUILDING

DAVID R. ERB, DMA

Except the Lord build the house,
they labor in vain that build it. –Psalm 127:1

Through wisdom a house is built,
and by understanding it is established. –Proverbs 24:3

The stone which the builders rejected
has become the chief cornerstone. –Psalm 118:22

To build a magnificent edifice that will last and glorify the Lord is a daunting task. When Solomon set out to build the temple as well as his own house, he employed Huram, the master craftsman from Tyre, who was not only skillful in his work, but filled with wisdom and understanding for such work.[1] Many things are necessary to complete such a task: God's blessing; a clear blueprint; the necessary time, materials, and tools; and a master builder. Many decisions, small

---

1. 1 Kings 7:13-14; 2 Chronicles 2:13-14.

and large, will need to be made along the way requiring discernment and discrimination. Such decisions must be made with the intent of making wise decisions after obtaining the requisite understanding. In most cases, there is not a single answer or a "one-size-fits-all" decision; however, there are certain principles which will apply to most situations.

God's Word provides many comparative models of wise and foolish building. This chapter purposes to take a biblically and historically Christian based look at the structuring of a good and faithful music program with a direct and pragmatic approach. It will do so in light of the biblical precept of making distinctions (i.e. good-bad, faithful-unfaithful, blessings-curses, mature-childish, etc.). This should not be considered an exclusive or exhaustive list of issues or ditches, but will hopefully address some of the most common areas of consideration. Negative models considered here are not meant to condemn nor insult schools who are presently employing such models; rather, the hope is to provide wise counsel in starting music programs or seeking to improve upon current practices with the knowledge that while the ideal is not always a reality in the present, it is nevertheless a goal to be striving toward into the future.

GOD'S BLESSING: PHILOSOPHY & FOUNDATION

Seeking God's blessing and will for our lives is something we ought to do no matter the endeavor. Before discussing curricular issues or the day-to-day execution of the plan, a proper foundation must be laid in accordance with God's plans. Perhaps the biggest issue for many ACCS schools is that despite being Christian and classical in name, the music program is not grounded in nor does it reflect historic Christian or classical teaching or pedagogy. A music program does not become Christian or classical just because we put our logo on it any more than a paper weight is made Christian by putting a cross on it.

God has implemented singing as a design feature in all His creation, most notably man. This is because God is a singer, and we are created in His image.[2] God has made us to be instruments of His praise. He has created singing to be the one of the primary means by which we are filled with His Word and Spirit.[3] Singing is required of us as much as, if not more than, any other imperative in the Bible.[4] Eschatologically, singing is one of the few things which we know we will be doing in heaven without a doubt.[5] If this is true, it would seem that music must be central to how we train up our children in the *paideia* of the Lord.

From a classical perspective, singing was viewed as one of the most primary means of forming the soul/character of man/society. Plato said:

> Education in music is most sovereign, because more than anything else rhythm and harmony find their way to the inmost soul and take strongest hold upon it, bringing with them and imparting grace, if only one is rightly trained, and otherwise the contrary.[6]

For the modes of music are never disturbed without unsettling of the most fundamental political and social conventions.[7]

---

2. Zephaniah 3:16.

3. Colossians 3:16-17; Ephesians 5:17-21.

4. The Book of Psalms, Isaiah, etc.

5. Revelation 4-5.

6. Oliver Strunk, *Source Readings in Music History: Antiquity and the Middle Ages* (New York: W. W. Norton & Company, 1965), 8.

7. Piero Weiss and Richard Taruskin, *Music in the Western World: A History in Documents* (Belmont: Thompson Schirmer, 2008), 7.

Centuries later, Quintilian said:

> If there were anything novel in my insistence on the study of music, I should have to treat the matter at greater length. But in view of the fact that the study of music has, from those remote times when Chiron taught Achilles down to our own day, continued to be studied by all except those who have a hatred for any regular course of study, it would be a mistake to seem to cast any doubt upon its value by showing an excessive zeal in its defense.[8]

Unfortunately, an excessive zeal is necessary today given the state of music education. Further study of Pythagoras, Boethius, the *Music of the Spheres*, the *Orpheus Myth*, and music as one of the four mathematical sciences of the quadrivium similarly leads us to the idea that the teaching of music must be central to how and why we train up our children.

Therefore our foundation must be purposefully Christian and classical all the way up and down. But the proof is in the pudding. Because most people have not grown up under this paradigm but rather under a public school model and in light of the fact that most administrators are not very advanced in their own musical training, it is a public school paradigm which most schools emulate by default. This can take various forms but some would include:

1. Viewing music as a non-core elective after elementary school. A biblical/historical-classical-Christian model does not formally conclude a musical education at the end of the grammar stage.
2. Viewing music, art, and drama as three equal "arts" choices. God calls all people to come before His presence with singing,

---

8. Ibid., 11.

not with music, art, or drama. Everyone is to sing God's praises, not everyone is summoned to paint or sculpt unto the Lord. While I am not at all opposed to training up everyone in these various arts, God does not call us to an arts-elective curriculum. His design places music as the central means to worship Him, teach and admonish one another, and proclaim His glory and gospel.

3. Performing music in a youth-only segregated manner. The biblical/historical-Christian model is the teacher *with* the student, the young *with* the old; it is a communal activity and one with various choirs brought together.[9] While there is need for systematic training along the way, and different levels are necessary, only singing with one's age group is not a good way to train up students in a *paideia* manner. Singing together, the young with the old, the parents with the children, etc. should be something we desire to encourage in various ways. Historic church choirs consisted of pre-pubescent boys and men singing the music of Palestrina, Byrd, Bach, and others.

The preceding models are neither biblical nor classical. In addition to being steeped in the teachings of the Bible and the ancient Greeks and Romans, the writings of Martin Luther are strong in their support of the centrality of music education:

> Necessity demands that music be kept in the schools. A schoolmaster must know how to sing; otherwise I do not look at him. And before a youth is ordained into the ministry, he should practice music in school.[10]

---

9. 1 Chronicles 25:8; Psalm 148:11-12.

10. Carl F. Schalk, *Luther on Music: Paradigms of Praise* (St. Louis: Concordia Publishing House, 1988), 30.

It is worth noting that Luther's comment is in reference to youth who would go on to "non-musical" vocations. The study of music is not only for those who will go on to teach and perform but for all people.

THE BLUEPRINT: PROGRAM STRUCTURE

If both form and content are crucial to a good result, then the structure of the music program must be considered just as much as the curriculum. These two areas must work together and not be at odds with one another in a "bricks without straw" sort of way. Below are four areas to consider.

Mandatory K-12 music

In light of the previous section, I see no other conclusion than requiring music instruction from kindergarten through the senior year. Why is it that the three "Rs" or Latin or STEM courses are all placed ahead of music in the queue of what is important/necessary? A quick Bible study on music versus a Bible study on math or a foreign language would leave an observer puzzled as to most schools' understanding of the Bible. While we all happily sing the concluding verse of "Amazing Grace," "We've no less days to *sing* God's praise than when we'd first begun," we design our school structure saying, "We've no less days to do advanced mathematics, Latin, etc." Music has a grammar, logic, and rhetoric which need to be seen all the way through. As mentioned above, requiring music in the grammar stage and then making it optional during the logic and rhetoric stages is just bad *telos*. We want our students to be able to interact with and perform music at the rhetorical level and enjoy its fruit. The state of music in western culture as well as the contemporary church displays a people whose music education is immature at best. If we want to change culture and grow up into musical maturity in Christ, then we need to see the instruction through in a classical-Christian way just as we do so many other areas of study.

Systematic Instruction

For the literacy and skill based portion of the instruction of music, separate class or grade instruction is necessary. Frequently, music is the only subject in which schools combine multiple grades (i.e. K-3, 6-12). Can you imagine teaching literature or math or anything else to a room of kindergarteners through third graders or sixth through twelfth graders all at the same time? Such a set up really contradicts the sequential, trivium-based approach to teaching.

Performing Ensembles

Performing ensembles (choir, band, orchestra) are different from music literacy classes just as literature or drama are different from grammar or composition classes. Can you imagine expecting all elements of English (grammar, writing, penmanship, literature, rhetoric, speech/debate, etc.) to be taught in one class (60-90 minutes tops) entitled "Drama" in which was also the expectation of producing a full scale play as well? Welcome to the world of your music teacher. Ensembles are entities in which some grade combination is possible (i.e. 2-3, 4-6, 7-8, 9-12). At the higher levels, multiple ensembles may be necessary to account for ability difference (i.e. honors/advanced ensembles). Performing ensembles should not really be a part of the lower elementary structure. The purpose of such ensembles is to perform written music which presupposes an ability to read the music. It is the equivalent of a literature or drama class. Students are not taught how to read in literature or drama classes, and such classes do not occur in the middle school or high school if the students cannot even read English. Therefore performing ensembles should be a more and more prominent part of the program as the students enter into the logic and rhetoric years having accumulated the necessary musical tools and the ability to use them.

A House Divided

I strongly suggest that a competing ensemble structure be avoided because such a model usually ends up with a good band and an anemic choir or vice versa. Ultimately, the choir will likely lose, as students who invest time and money into instrumental lessons will choose band; thus the more skillful/advanced musicians will be found in the instrumental ensemble. While singing is primary biblically, we do see that the singing is almost always accompanied with instruments. The musical Levites both sang and played musical instruments. I suggest that it would be best to set things up so that students can do both (i.e. Choir M/W, Band/Orchestra T/R, Theory F). While this might result in less time than both the choir and band director would want for their respective ensembles, the improved musicianship in the students as a result of such a structure would greatly benefit the students' skill and efficiency.

TIME, TOOLS, & MATERIALS: THE CURRICULUM

Most serious core-subject classes are given a good amount of time for the teaching of its curriculum. Four to five full length class times during the week are normative. Such classes are notable for a well thought out systematic and sequential curriculum. These classes also are usually supplied with the necessary tools/equipment/materials (i.e. literature books, composition paper, microscopes, etc.). And unique subjects such as science, art, or physical education often have their own dedicated spaces. For many music programs, most of these elements are not present. It need not be this way, of course, and while there are many reasons such situations are so prevalent, the bottom line is that a clear curriculum, a logical pedagogy, adequate time, tools, and materials are necessary for everything we teach in our schools—music included.

Here are some things to consider:

1. **LITERACY.** The music curriculum should be literacy based at its core, not concert based. Concerts are indeed glorious events and the culmination of much hard work; however, concerts should not be allowed to become the tail which wags the dog. A strong literacy program will culminate in beautifully skillful concerts. It is not necessarily true that good ensemble programs are made up of literate performers. The purpose of learning a language is to achieve full literacy: the ability to read, write, speak, and comprehend with skill and understanding. This is no different in English, Latin, or Music. As a language, the teaching and learning of Music is well suited to the structure of the Trivium: (1) *Grammar*—learning the basic structural elements of music (rhythm, melody, harmony, timbre, texture, form, dynamics), (2) *Dialectic*—learning how the elements are used to create music (i.e. music theory), and (3) *Rhetoric*—learning how to assess/perform/create music skillfully and with understanding.[11] In order to achieve such literacy, music twice a week for 30 minutes each is just not sufficient. Daily instruction is needed.

2. **STEADFAST COMMITMENT.** A long-game commitment to a tried and true approach to music education should be present. A program cannot flourish if the curriculum is unclear, or is a potpourri approach, or changes every time a new teacher is hired. It is not because there is only one approach that is the best (although there are more

---

11. David R. Erb, "Sing with Understanding, Play Skillfully: Musical Literacy for All the Saints," in *Teaching Beauty: A Vision for Music & Art in Christian Education*, ed. by G. Tyler Fischer with Ned Bustard (Baltimore: Square Halo Books, 2016), 125.

bad approaches than good ones), but if we are curricularly "tossed to and fro and carried about"[12] with every new teacher or faddish music gimmick then we should at the very least stop advertising that we are Christian and classical in our teaching of music. Such a commitment must flow from kindergarten through twelfth grade, from recorder class to choir to band to orchestra. Obviously different teachers will do things in different ways. High school orchestra is different than second grade music, but if one teacher teaches Kodály, and the next Orff, and the next only does music appreciation, the program will never flourish. Simply stated, I would recommend the Kodály approach for K-6 and a classical literature approach for 7-12. There is much to be fleshed out here, but this is not within the scope of this chapter.

3. **BE DOERS, NOT APPRECIATORS ONLY.** Usually when a music appreciation class is offered, that is code for "a music class which purposes *not* to teach you to be doers or makers of music, but sideline spectators only." Such classes are typically for the non-musicians who are not in choir or band. They are taught facts about composers and play "drop the needle." Again, do we do this with other classes? Math appreciation? Latin appreciation? Physical education appreciation? Are you laughing yet? Generally speaking, people who can actually do something well and with understanding appreciate it more than those who have no actual skill and only tangential understanding. This is not to suggest that teaching facts about composers or historical eras or musical genres is to be avoided. Not at all. It would

---

12. Ephesians 4:14.

just be better to tie it in with the actual performing of music whether in music classes or in ensembles.

4. QUALITY LITERATURE. The music literature which we choose to study and perform should be of high quality, most of which is from the past and has stood the test of time. The music should exhibit an aesthetic of truth, goodness, and beauty: Bach, not Beyoncé; Palestrina, not Petra; Michael Praetorius, not Michael W. Smith. One of the primary tenets of Zoltán Kodály's approach to music education is "that only music of unquestioned quality—both folk and composed—should be used in the education of children."[13] While age/skill appropriateness is necessary, there is a difference between quality music for children and the bulk of composed children's music today. Remember that the great music written by Palestrina, Tallis, Bach, and others was written to be performed on a daily/weekly basis by pre-pubescent boys and men. The music we choose (and I mean music, not the lyrics—that is another matter) ought to be comparable to the literature which we choose; it should be worthy of our time, study and affection. Trivial, cheesy, banal, sentimental, or contemporary/popular music is not worthy of our dedicated study and *paideia* education. At the end of the day, musically speaking, you are what you sing. Do you sing mainly jazz? Then you are a jazz choir. Do you sing mainly madrigals? Then you are a madrigal choir. Do you mainly sing contemporary Christian praise and worship music? Then you are a Christian

---

13. Lois Choksy, *The Kodály Context: Creating an Environment for Musical Learning* (Englewood Cliffs: Prentice-Hall, 1981), 8.

pop choir. Do you mainly sing music by the masters? Then you are a classical concert choir.

5. GOD'S WORD. Singing God's Word should be our primary song literature, particularly for our more advanced choral ensembles. Biblical psalms, canticles, and pericopes ought to be our main fare. In principle, no one would object to this; however, in practice most Christians and most churches, and as a result most Christian schools, sing a much greater percentage of man's words than God's Word. Now I am not at all against singing good Christian poetry, but if it supplants the Word of God in our affections then it has become an idol. Creeds and catechisms are wonderful things, but they are not the Word of God. Augustine and Calvin are definitely worth reading, but they are not Scripture. "Amazing Grace" and "When I Survey the Wondrous Cross" are wonderful hymns and have been a blessing to thousands of Christians, but they are not the songs of David. So many Christians know and love at least 40-60 hymns but sadly could not sing perhaps more than one or two of God's 150 Psalms. Again, the point is not that we must choose to sing only Scripture, but if we had to choose, the choice is clear. How much Scripture would dwell in our students after thirteen years of instruction if only we taught them to sing it as God has instructed us.[14]

MASTER BUILDERS: STAFFING

Staffing is really the most important consideration of all. Ultimately, who we hire to teach our children music is more important than all other considerations. If it is true that a student will be like his

---

14. Colossians 3:16.

teacher (Luke 6:40), and it is, then we must hire skillful musicians who are also skillful teachers. Unfortunately, this is the point right out of the gate at which many schools fall.

Chenaniah

In 1 Chronicles 15ff in which King David establishes the Tabernacle in Jerusalem, one of the things he does is to set up the musical aspect of the worship:

> Then David spoke to the leaders of the Levites to appoint their brethren to be the singers accompanied by instruments of music, stringed instruments, harps, and cymbals, by raising the voice with resounding joy. So the Levites appointed Heman... Asaph...(and) Ethan (Jeduthun). Chenaiah, leader of the Levites, was instructor in charge of the music, because he was skillful.[15]

Later in 1 Chronicles 25 we read that not only were Chenaniah, Heman, Asaph, and Jeduthun skillful in music, but so too were all their many brethren who were likewise instructed in music:

> All these were under the direction of their father for the music in the house of the Lord, with cymbals, stringed instruments, and harps, for the service of the House of God. Asaph, Jeduthun, and Heman were under the authority of the king. So the number of them, with their brethren who were instructed in the songs of the Lord, all who were skillful, was two hundred and eighty-eight.[16]

---

15. 1 Chronicles 15:16-22.
16. 1 Chronicles 25:6-7.

Here we have a biblical model for musicians and the teachers/leaders thereof. Here we have biblical-musical fathers: Chenaniah, Heman, Asaph, and Jeduthun. All music teachers should strive to walk in their steps, and all administrators should seek to hire such skillful music teachers.

First Law of Teaching

John Milton Gregory's *Seven Laws of Teaching* begins with the following cornerstone law: "A teacher must be one who knows the lesson or truth to be taught."[17] Later he says that "The unknowing teacher is the blind trying to lead the blind with only an empty lamp to lead the way." [18]

Kodály famously noted that:

> It is more important who the singing master at Kisvárda is than who the director of the Opera House is, because a poor director will fail. [Often even a good one.] But a bad teacher may kill the love of music for thirty years in thirty classes of pupils.[19]

Alas, how true and how sadly this is often the case. Once Kodály's method was officially adopted in Hungary, it was only implemented in a new school when a qualified teacher was available. This slow yet principled obedience to this primary truth resulted in an amazing transformation. In the span of one lifetime an entire nation matured from musical illiteracy to musical literacy.

---

17. John Milton Gregory, *The Seven Laws of Teaching* (Moscow, ID: Charles Nolan Publishers, 2003), 19.

18. Ibid., 30.

19. Lois Choksy, *The Kodály Method II: Folksong to Masterwork* (Upper Saddle River: Prentice-Hall, 1999), 3.

Lois Choksy describes the situation in Hungary:

> Music seems to be part of the very fiber of Hungarian life. Hungary, a nation the size of Indiana, with a population of ten million people, has eight hundred adult concert choirs, fifty of the first rank and another hundred of radio or public performance quality. There are four professional symphony orchestras in Budapest alone and five in country towns, as well as numerous amateur orchestras. A person without a musical education is considered illiterate. Almost all play instruments; almost all sing. Concert halls are full.
>
> The situation was not always so. Early in the 1900s, Zoltán Kodály, the noted Hungarian composer and educator, was appalled at the level of musical literacy he found in students entering the Zeneakadémia— the highest music school in Hungary. Not only were these students unable to read and write music fluently, but in addition, they were totally ignorant of their own musical heritage.[20]

There are no two ways about it: schools must seek to hire skillful, vocationally trained music teachers if they wish to have a biblically mature music program. The long-term plan cannot be to keep plugging in low-budget solutions by employing someone who took piano and sang in choir twenty to forty years ago. I do not say this to disparage those endeavoring to work faithfully in the situation they find themselves. Not at all. You do not blame the violinist for not being a good oboe teacher, nor the pianist for not being a good choir director. One cannot

---

20. Lois Choksy, *The Kodály Method I: Comprehensive Music Education, Third Edition* (Upper Saddle River: Prentice Hall, 2000), 1.

teach what they do not know nor were equipped to do. If indeed the "Law of the Teacher" is foundational as well as biblical and classical then we need to be serious about training up and hiring properly trained musicians to fill the void.

MISCELLANEOUS

Having touched upon four major categories, I find many other things to consider as schools endeavor to implement or improve upon their music program. Here are a few items:

1. Don't do or not do music because you do or do not happen to have a music teacher. This pragmatic approach will lead to the school focusing on music or drama or art or Spanish depending on who happens to blow through the school. Do or don't do music because you philosophically believe you should (or shouldn't).

2. Administrators ought to be mindful of the differences between teaching music and other subjects. Don't just count minutes. How many other teachers teach every student in your school? Are any other teachers responsible for putting on concerts, etc. as part of their curricular classes?

3. When making plans for the music program, consult your music teachers as well as other seasoned music teachers. Non-musical administrators and board members often make well-intentioned, yet uninformed decisions when it comes to music programs. There is no need to reinvent the wheel. If you set out to build a new school building, you will no doubt consider various examples of building designs both good and bad, consult with skillful architects, and hire a master builder. The same ought to apply when building a music program.

4. Work toward creating dedicated and appropriate music facilities. Not the gym stage with PE going on below. Not the lunch room with students having study hall and teachers having conversations. Invest in good instruments (i.e. pianos, xylophones, recorders, etc.) and not the cheapest option available. You cannot make beautiful music surrounded by noise and with dilapidated instruments.

5. If you are going to put on concerts, consider finding a venue with a space and an acoustic suitable to performing classical music (i.e. not a gym, theater, or modern church). Provide adequate rehearsal time in the performance space accounting for both logistics and rehearsing the music. Plan the budget adequately accounting for space rental, instrumentalists, and other items.

6. Work to change the lay of the land between sports and music. Keep them from being adversaries. Set them up to complement one another in a proper and balanced way. I love sports and am a big fan, but it is all too common that sports programs and schedules end up dominating many schools. Music classes often get scheduled during last period, and then students miss the class to leave early to make it to away games. Games and concerts get scheduled on top of one another. While there are many parallels between them, sports are games whereas music is a calling upon all people on the earth. Let's change the refrain from "I can't, I have practice" to "I can't, I have rehearsal."

If your music program was a building, what kind of building would it be? A portable all-purpose classroom? A multi-purpose cafetorium? A glorious cathedral with beautiful visual aesthetics and aural acoustics designed for the worship of the most high God? If we do not really know what we want we are certain not to get it. If we do know what we want then we need to start building in such a way that will get us to the desired result. Like Kodály in Hungary, I believe that the ACCS is uniquely positioned to effect notable cultural changes in our land. In order to achieve this we must first seek God and His will and then endeavor to execute His blueprints. Psalm 67 opens with a prayer for God's blessing so that His way and His salvation would be known throughout earth. At the end of the Psalm we see the prayer fulfilled with blessings and salvation extending to the ends of the earth. At the center of the chiastic psalm is the means to the end:

> Let the peoples praise You, O God;
> > Let all the peoples praise You.
> > > Oh, let the nations be glad and sing for joy!
> > > > For You shall judge the people righteously,
> > > > And govern the nations on earth.
> > > Let the peoples praise You, O God;
> > Let all the peoples praise You.[21]

Truly this kind of building project will last much longer than any of our brick and mortar edifices. We are teaching and training up our children who, like us, are temples of God.[22] Such temples are to be filled with the Word and Spirit of God.[23] So let's get building! And may we through God's grace build wisely. *Soli Deo Gloria!*

---

21. Psalm 67:3-5.

22. 1 Corinthians 3:16-17.

23. Colossians 3:16; Ephesians 5:18.

7

RESOURCE RECOMMENDATIONS

DAVID ERB & JARROD RICHEY

PRIMARY SCHOOL CURRICULAR SUGGESTIONS

Singing is the gateway to music literacy and advanced musicianship endeavors, and a good collection of songs will serve the music teacher well. This is by no means an exhaustive list but more of a recommended resource list for teachers and administrators. The hope is that this chapter will make it easier for the teacher to locate quality music literacy-driven resources both old and new.

SONG READERS AND COLLECTIONS

There are numerous anthologies out there that can provide reading material and practice material for your students. Many of these books have overlapping song material, yet they are each useful tools to have in your library. These song collections will give you reading material for your students to use in classroom instruction as well as performance and game activity. The materials are not necessarily structured by grade, and you will find things in each that can be used in most elementary and middle school grades. These materials will provide both new and review material to read in the general music classroom.

> Bacon, Denise. *46 Two-part American Folk Songs: For Elementary Grades*. Wellesley, MA: Kodály Center of America, 1973.
>
> Bacon, Denise. *50 Easy Two-part Exercises*. First Steps in Singing. Wellesley, MA: Kodály Center of America, 1977.
>
> Bacon, Denise. *185 Unison Pentatonic Exercises*. First Steps in Singing. Wellesley, MA: Kodály Center of America, 1978.
>
> Bolkovac, Edward, and Judith Johnson. *150 Rounds for Singing and Teaching*. New York: Boosey & Hawkes, 1996.
>
> Choksy, Lois, and David Brummitt. *120 Singing Games and Dances for Elementary Schools*. Englewood Cliffs, NJ: Prentice-Hall, 1987.
>
> Crowe, Edgar, Annie Lawton, and W. Gillies. Whittaker. *The Folk Song Sight Singing Series*. London: Oxford University Press, 1970.
>
> Erdei, Ida, Faith Knowles, and Denise Bacon, eds. *My Singing Bird: 150 Songs from the Anglo-American, African-American, English, Scottish, and Irish Traditions*. Columbus, OH: Kodály Center of America, 2002.
>
> Erdei, Péter, and Katalin Komlós. *150 American Folk Songs to Sing, Read and Play*. New York: Boosey & Hawkes, 1974.
>
> Feierabend, John M. *The Book of Echo Songs: I'll Sing After You*. Chicago: GIA Publications, 2003.

Feierabend, John M. *The Book of Canons. First Steps in Music*. Chicago: GIA Publications, 2014.

Johnston, Richard. *Folk Songs North America Sings: A Source Book for All Teachers*. Toronto: E. C. Kerby, 1984.

Kodály, Zoltán. *333 Reading Exercises*. London: Boosey & Hawkes, 1972.

Kodály, Zoltán. *Bicinia Hungarica*. Revised English ed. 4 vols. London: Boosey & Hawkes, 1968.

Kodály, Zoltán. *Fifteen Two-part Exercises*. London: Boosey & Hawkes., 1952.

Locke, Eleanor, comp. *Sail Away: 155 American Folk Songs to Sing, Read and Play*. Edited by Peter Erdei. New York: Boosey & Hawkes, 2000.

Agócsy, László. *Classical Canons - 230 Solfeggio*. Edited by Antal Molnar. Editio Musica Budapest, 1955.

The Kings Singers: Book of Rounds, Canons and Partsongs. Milwaukee: Hal Leonard Corporation, 2002.

Locke, Eleanor G., comp. *Sail Away: 155 American Folk Songs to Sing, Read and Play*. Edited by Peter Erdei. New York: Boosey & Hawkes, 1981.

The Kings Singers: Book of Rounds, Canons and Partsongs. Milwaukee: Hal Leonard Corporation, 2002.

Wilson, Harry R., comp. *Old and New Rounds and Canons*. Delaware Water Gap, PA: Harold Flammer, 1967.

KODÁLY METHODOLOGY RESOURCES

The following resources provide both a sequence of concepts and instruction in how to teach from a Kodály approach. Much like a Physician's Desk Reference or WebMD, these resources are best when paired with training and apprenticeship in this approach. The following texts will come alive through workshops and specific training classes in summer course certification.

> Brumfield, Susan. *First, We Sing!: Kodály-inspired Teaching for the Music Classroom.* Milwaukee, WI: Hal Leonard Corporation, 2014.
>
> Choksy, Lois. *The Kodály Method I: Comprehensive Music Education.* Upper Saddle River, NJ: Prentice Hall, 1999.
>
> Choksy, Lois. *Kodály Method II: Folksong to Masterwork.* Upper Saddle River, NJ: Prentice-Hall, 1999.
>
> Dániel, Katinka Scipiades., and Zoltán Kodály. *Kodály Approach: Method Book.* 3 vols. Belmont, CA: Lear Siegler,/Fearon Publishers, 1973.
>
> Dániel, Katinka Scipiades. *Kodály in Kindergarten: 50 Lesson Plans, Curriculum, Song Collection.* Nashville: Fostco Music Press, 1981.
>
> Eisen, Ann, and Lamar Robertson. *Yearly Plans: For Coordinated Use with An American Methodology.* Lake Charles, LA: Sneaky Snake Publications, 2009.
>
> Eisen, Ann, and Lamar Robertson. *An American Methodology: An Inclusive Approach to Musical Literacy.* Lake Charles, LA.: Sneaky Snake Publications, 2010.

Eisen, Ann, and Lamar Robertson. *From Folk Songs to Masterworks: Art Music Listening Lessons for Grades K-6*. Lake Charles, LA: Sneaky Snake Publications, 2010.

Katalin, Forrai. *Music in Preschool*. Translated by Jean Sinor. Revised ed. Brisbane, Australia: Clayfield School of Music, 1998.

Houlahan, Mícheál, and Philip Tacka. *Kodály Today: A Cognitive Approach to Elementary Music Education*. New York: Oxford University Press, 2008.

Szönyi, Erzsébet. *Kodály's Principles in Practice*. London: Boosey & Hawkes, 1973.

SECONDARY CHORAL CURRICULAR SUGGESTIONS

To begin with, it must be pointed out that there is no curriculum proper for a choral ensemble; there is no musical equivalent to Saxon Math or omnibus. It is similar to a great books approach except that choirs do not sing the same music every year like teachers go through the same books every year with the senior literature class. As such, the literature is always changing. This can make it difficult for teachers without years of training and experience.

While there is no curriculum proper, one can set up principles and paradigms to guide literature selection, vocal technique, and musicianship training. There are many books and videos available to assist in these areas. While this list of resources contains a wealth of information to help one learn the craft of conducting, I should caution that these are no substitute for mentoring under master teachers/ conductors and singing in and listening to many good choirs. People would not choose a pilot or surgeon who has only read a few books on their respective subjects. The same standard should be applied to the choir director even if it is not a matter of life and death.

Singing in good choirs that sing good or great literature will provide interaction with good or great choral literature. Buying scores and playing through them will help a director tangibly learn the literature. Buying CDs and listening to learn repertoire, style, and sound quality is formative. Observing conductors and listening to live choirs, good and bad, is invaluable. Attending choral conferences, studying conducting, choral literature, music theory, music history, aural skills, Dalcroze Eurhythmics, voice, piano, etc. are ultimately necessary if one really wants to be a choral conductor. Without such knowledge and tools the school is left with a music teacher who can teach parts but is unlikely to build or inspire choir unto beautiful and joyful music making. Nevertheless, there is much here to be of great help and point you in the right direction.

Choral Literature

My suggestions on this topic are:

1. make sure you are spending most of your time singing the music of the masters.[1] While you will likely be unable to access the greatest works of such composers, they all have more easily accessible music. I would also encourage you to learn to adapt and arrange good music by master composers for your ensembles. Don't settle for modern cheap and easy

---

1. des Prez, Lassus, Palestrina, Victoria, Sweelinck, Tallis, Byrd, Weelkes, Gibbons, Gabrieli, Monteverdi, Schuetz, Scheidt, Schein, Praetorius, Pachelbel, Buxtehude, Bach, Purcell, Vivaldi, Handel, Haydn, Mozart, Billings, Schubert, Beethoven, Mendelssohn, Brahms, Faure, Durufle, Vaughan Williams, Copland, Thompson, Britten, etc.

compositions and arrangements from the major publishers who toss out bad music like chum to the sharks. Instead, search reputable music publishers.[2]

2. In addition to focusing on master composers, make sure you are regularly covering the main choral genres: motets, cantatas, oratorios, full anthems, verse anthems, fuging tunes, spirituals, chorales, chorale-motets, historic hymnody, historic psalmody, madrigals, folk song arrangements, etc.

Benedictines of Solesmes, editors. *The Liber Usualis*. Great Falls, MO: St. Bonaventure Publications, 1997.

Choral Public Domain Library. http://www.cpdl.org/wiki/.

Drinker, Sophie. *Brahms and his Women's Choruses*. Merion, PA: Musurgia Publishers, 1952.

Dürr, Alfred. *The Cantatas of J. S. Bach*. New York, NY: Oxford University Press, 2005.

IMSLP Petrucci Music Library. https://imslp.org/.

Knapp, J. Merrill. *Selected List of Music for Men's Voices*. Princeton, NJ: Princeton University Press, 1952.

Laster, James. *Catalogue of Choral Music Arranged in Biblical Order*. Metuchen, NJ: Scarecrow Press, Inc., 1983.

Locke, Arthur Ware & Fassett, Charles K. *Selected List of Choruses for Women's Voices*. Northampton, MA: Smith College, 1965.

Robinson, Ray, editor. *Choral Music: A Norton Historical Anthology*. New York, NY: W. W. Norton & Company, Inc., 1978.

---

2. Oxford, Carus, Concordia, Bärenreiter, Breitkopf und Härtel, Augsburg, G. Schirmer, Boosey & Hawkes, GIA, etc.

Schrock, Dennis. *Choral Repertoire.* New York, NY: Oxford University Press, 2009.

Unger, Melvin P. *Handbook to Bach's Sacred Cantata Texts.* Lanham, MD: Scarecrow Press, Inc., 1996.

Young, Percy M. *The Choral Tradition: A historical and analytical survey from the sixteenth century to the present day.* New York, NY: W. W. Norton & Company, Inc., 1981.

Choral Pedagogy

Finding good literature is relatively easy compared to learning how to train and prepare your choir, to develop their sound, to improve their musicianship, and how to run and structure rehearsals. Below are various resources which address these most important issues.

Chafe, Eric. *Analyzing Bach Cantatas.* New York, NY: Oxford University Press, 2000.

Ehmann, Wilhelm & Haasemann, Frauke. *Voice Building for Choirs.* Chapel Hill, NC: Hinshaw Music Inc., 1981.

Haasemann, Frauke & Jordan, Frauke. *Group Vocal Technique.* Chapel Hill, NC: Hinshaw Music Inc., 1991.

Jordan, James. *Evoking Sound: Fundamentals of Choral Conducting.* Chicago, IL: GIA Publications, Inc., 2009.

Jordan, James. *Evoking Sound: The Choral Rehearsal, Volume One, Techniques and Procedures; A Comprehensive Rehearsal Technique Sourcebook.* Chicago, IL: GIA Publications, Inc., 2007.

Jordan, James. *Evoking Sound: The Choral Rehearsal, Volume Two, Inward Bound; Philosophy and Score Preparation.* Chicago, IL: GIA Publications, Inc., 2008.

Mann, Alfred. *Bach and Handel: Choral Performance Practice.* Chapel Hill, NC: Hinshaw Music Inc., 1992.

Noble, Weston. *Achieving Choral Blend Through Standing Position DVD.* Chicago, IL: GIA Publications, Inc., 2005.

O'Toole, Patricia. *Shaping Sound Musicians: An Innovative Approach to Teaching Comprehensive Musicianship Through Performance.* Chicago, IL: GIA Publications, Inc., 2003.

Stapert, Calvin R. *Handel's Messiah: Comfort for God's People.* Grand Rapids, MI: William B. Eerdmans Publishing Company, 2010.

Stapert, Calvin R. *My Only Comfort: Death, Deliverance, and Discipleship in the Music of Bach.* Grand Rapids, MI: William B. Eerdmans Publishing Company, 2000.

Van Camp, Leonard. *A Practical Guide for Performing, Teaching and Singing "Messiah."* Dayton, OH: Roger Dean Publishing Company, 1993.

Conducting

The art of conducting is different than teaching vocal parts, the structure and style of the music, or shaping the sound of a choir. There are many skillful musicians who can do such things but then cannot conduct their way out of a paper sack. Choral conductors often are known for not being able to keep a basic pattern, for having limp-wristed and unclear gestures, and directly contradicting their verbal instruction with the communication of their hands. Even when learning a decent technique, the conductor hasn't learned how to lead and inspire large groups of people to bring the music to life in a beautifully rhetorical manner. The following resources address such matters as far as books are able to do so.

Beck, Joseph G. *America's Choral Ambassador John Finley Williamson: Founder of the world famous Westminster Choir.* Bloomington, IN: AuthorHouse, 2014.

Decker, Harold A. & Herford, Julius. *Choral Conducting Symposium.* Englewood Cliffs, NJ: Prentice Hall, 1988.

Ehmann, Wilhelm. *Choral Directing.* Minneapolis, MN: Augsburg Publishing House, 1968.

Finn, William J. *The Art of the Choral Conductor, Volume I.* Evanston, IL: Summy-Birchard Publishing Company, 1939.

Fowler, Charles, eds. *Conscience of a Profession: Howard Swan Choral Director and Teacher.* Chapel Hill, NC: Hinshaw Music Inc., 1987.

Green, Elizabeth A. H. *The Modern Conductor.* Upper Saddle River, NJ: Prentice Hall, 1997.

Moses, Don V., Robert W. Demaree, and Allen F. Ohmes. *Face to Face with Orchestra and Chorus: A Handbook for Choral Conductors.* Bloomington: Indiana University Press, 2004.

Nally, Donald. *Conversations with Joseph Flummerfelt: Thoughts on Conducting, Music, and Musicians.* Lanham, MD: Scarecrow Press, Inc., 2010.

Shaw, Robert. *Preparing a Masterpiece DVDs (8 volumes).* New York, NY: Carnegie Hall; available on YouTube.

Webb, Guy B., eds. *Up Front: Becoming the Complete Choral Conductor.* Boston, MA: ECS Publishing, 1993.

Miscellaneous Resources

The following resources cover many different areas: diction, translation, chant, vocal technique, professional choral organizations, and more.

>Alderson, Richard. *Complete Handbook of Voice Training.* West Nyack, NY: Parker Publishing Company, Inc., 1988.
>
>American Choral Directors Association: https://acda.org/
>
>Blocker, Robert, ed. *The Robert Shaw Reader.* New York, NY: Yale University Press, 2004.
>
>Burris, Keith C. *Deep River: The Life and Music of Robert Shaw.* Chicago, IL: GIA Publications, Inc., 2013.
>
>Dulas, Rev. Dcn. Jerald P. *The Psalter and the Canticles of the New King James Version: Set to the Gregorian Psalm Tones in Modern Notation and Supplied with Appropriate Antiphons.* Malone, TX: Repristination Press, 2012.
>
>Jeffers, Ron. *Translations and Annotations of Choral Repertoire Volume I: Sacred Latin Texts.* Corvallis, OR: Earthsongs, 1988.
>
>Jeffers, Ron. *Translations and Annotations of Choral Repertoire Volume II: German Texts.* Corvallis, OR: Earthsongs, 2000.
>
>Jeffers, Ron. *Translations and Annotations of Choral Repertoire Volume III: French and Italian Texts.* Corvallis, OR: Earthsongs, 2007.
>
>Jeffers, Ron. *Translations and Annotations of Choral Repertoire Volume IV: Hebrew Texts.* Corvallis, OR: Earthsongs, 2009.

Linklater, Kristin. *Freeing the Natural Voice.* New York, NY: Drama Book Publishers, 1976.

Litton, James, ed. *The Plainsong Psalter.* New York, NY: Church Publishing Inc., 1988.

McKenzie, Duncan. *Training the Boy's Changing Voice.* New Brunswick, NJ: Rutgers University Press, 1956.

Moriarty, John. *Diction: Italian, Latin, French, German...the sounds and 81 exercises for singing them.* Boston, MA: E. C. Schirmer Music Company, 1975.

Tortolano, William. *A Gregorian Chant Handbook.* Chicago, IL: GIA Publications, Inc., 2005.

Wyton, Alec, ed. *The Anglican Chant Psalter.* New York, NY: Church Publishing Inc., 1987.

Biblical Worldview, Philosophy, Aesthetics

Developing a grounded and thorough biblical worldview and philosophy of music and aesthetics can transform not only what you do, but how and why you do it. Here are some books for starters.

Begbie, Jeremy S. *Resounding Truth: Christian Wisdom in the World of Music.* Grand Rapids, MI: Baker Academic, 2007.

Fischer, G. Tyler, ed. *Teaching Beauty: A Vision for Music & Art in Christian Education.* Baltimore, MD: Square Halo Books, 2016.

Gordon, T. David. *Why Johnny Can't Sing Hymns: How Pop Culture Rewrote the Hymnal.* Phillipsburg, NJ: P&R Publishing Company, 2010.

Johannson, Calvin M. *Music & Ministry: A Biblical Counterpoint.* Peabody, MA: Hendrickson Publishers, Inc., 1998.

Johannson, Calvin M. *Discipling Music Ministry: Twenty-first Century Directions.* Peabody, MA: Hendrickson Publishers, Inc., 1992.

Jones, Paul S. *Singing and Making Music: Issues in Church Music Today.* Phillipsburg, NJ: P & R Publishing Company, 2006.

Lefebvre, Michael. *Singing the Songs of Jesus: Revisiting the Psalms.* Scotland: Christian Focus Publications, Ltd., 2011.

Leupold, Ulrich S. editor. *Luther's Works Volume 53.* Philadelphia, PA: Fortress Press, 1965.

Schalk, Carl F. *Luther on Music: Paradigms of Praise.* St. Louis, MO: Concordia Publishing House, 1988.

Scruton, Roger. *The Aesthetics of Music.* New York, NY: Oxford University Press, 1999.

Scruton, Roger. *Understanding Music: Philosophy and Interpretation.* New York, NY: Continuum International Publishing Group, 2009.

Stapert, Calvin R. *A New Song for an Old World: Musical Thought in the Early Church.* Grand Rapids, MI: William B. Eerdmans Publishing Company, 2007.

Westermeyer, Paul. *Te Deum: The Church and Music.* Minneapolis, MN: Fortress Press, 1998.

Wright, N. T. *The Case for the Psalms: Why They Are Essential.* New York: Harper Collins, 2016.

Parent and Homeschool General Reading

Sometimes it is parents who want to be encouraged in how to better regard music education in their church, school, and local community. These resources provide a variety of helpful tools for parents and interested laymen.

> Drake, Joshua F. *Recovering Music Education as a Christian Liberal Art*. Mountain Home, AR: BorderStone Press, 2010.
>
> Fischer, G. Tyler, ed. *Teaching Beauty: A Vision for Music &; Art in Christian Education*. Baltimore, MD: Square Halo Books, 2016.
>
> Froehlich, Mary Ann. *Music Education in the Christian Home: The Complete Guide*. Brentwood, TN: Wolgemuth & Hyatt, 1990.
>
> Myers, Ken. *All Gods Children and Blue Suede Shoes: Christians & Popular Culture*. Wheaton, IL: Crossway, 1989.
>
> Richey, Jarrod. *Bach to the Future: Fostering Music Literacy Today*. Monroe, LA: Retune Publications, 2016.
>
> Wilson, Douglas. *Church Music and Other Kinds: A Musical Manifesto of Sorts*. Moscow, ID: Canon Press, 2014.

APPENDIX

To the Administrator

DAVID GOODWIN

The music teacher's work is mostly limited to the classroom, leaving the heads of each school to hire the music teachers, structure the programs, set the requirements, and evaluate the program's students and results. The administrators are responsible for bringing every program and activity under the larger vision of the school. This chapter is dedicated to helping school administrators create excellent music programs within their classical schools.

PRIORITY

Schools within the progressive education model tend to ignore the value of incorporating art and music studies in the schedule—particularly when factors like budgeting, standardized testing, or STEM apply pressure to the school system. For classical Christian schools, music is key, whether studying the muses of the Greeks or the psalmists of the Hebrews. Of course, music is a key part of the Christian identity, too. Christians need unique training because the unique call in our lives is to be worshippers. Because Christians are called to make melody with our whole heart, music should be more prevalent in our schools than in any other type of school. The question is how to rightly order our priorities for music while considering the other aims of classical Christian education.

TIME

There are about six to seven academic hours in a day. Math and science usually consume two hours. Reading, history, philosophy, theology, and language are often squeezed into the remaining four to five hours. There also are other special courses or electives. What's to be done? Anything I recommend involves a trade-off, one that is open for debate given the unique circumstances facing each school. That's the nature of time. There is no formula for the trade-offs, but there are right principles.

Music should ideally represent three periods or meetings a week. We need to give music more time than the other arts, especially in the younger grades, stealing time from science courses or other informational subjects if needed. Many ACCS schools make choir required through high school, often between three and five hours a week. If instrumental work is undertaken, a possible goal is the participation of a majority of students in an orchestra, or perhaps the requirement of one or two years of orchestra participation between 4th grade and 7th grade.

Schools can use their weekly music study periods wisely, or not. If song selection and pedagogy are weak or aligned with the music instruction of progressive education programs, the music study period will not be worth the investment. I would advise structuring a music program to complement the staff who are already available before seeking to expand.

APPENDIX: TO THE ADMINISTRATOR

CONTENT

Discernment will guide the formation of music schools. For example, do not underestimate what level of rigorous music training the children can handle. Progressive education programs encourage teachers to engage students with songs they like that are immediately accessible to them. Progressive academia is narrowing its music selections to the new music styles and compositions, dismissing the treasury of the past. Students may be fond of these new pieces because of the new pieces' similarities to pop music styles and themes, but students will not develop a long-term appreciation for great music made by the skilled composers of previous eras. This is not to say that folk music or popular music is never appropriate. Put another way, a teacher at a progressive education institution might use a Nancy Drew novel for instruction, whereas the classical educator should first look to the great novels. Clearly, course content selection is not a minor consideration.

In the earliest grades, students can learn simple folk songs and games to help them develop initial singing and music-making skills. By the mid-grammar stage, students can advance to more complex forms of music-making. Classical Christian schools can access a wealth of great sacred music, classical music, and original works of various genres like jazz, blues, and folk. Hymns are a good starting place to quickly get students singing regularly. Many schools have a "hymn of the month" to help students develop a repertoire of excellent hymns. For orchestras, there are many great works to be performed, and the occasional popular piece or simplified piece can be a hook to introduce students to this forgotten form of music-making. Many schools rarely attempt teaching complex musical compositions because the skill required to master such complex music is difficult to attain. And, nobody enjoys doing music poorly—especially children.

FACULTY

At schools within the progressive education system, music education degrees are the staple of the music classroom. In classical Christian schools, music performance majors are more likely to be the ones engaged in teaching music. Both of these backgrounds can be problematic. Teaching music to children is both an art and a skill. Knowing about music is not a sufficient qualification for teaching children, but the mere ability to play an instrument or sing is not a sufficient qualification either. In addition, instrumental teachers are often overly attached to band. The music of the string ensemble is going to be more complex and layered than that of the pep or marching band, making it hard for such teachers to transition to teaching music for the string ensemble or other types of music that pre-date marching band music. Music performance majors and the music education majors should be re-oriented to the principles of music instruction offered in this book.

VISION

You may not think you need a new vision for what your classical school's music program could look like. Your school's ensembles may participate in local and state festivals and honor choirs right on par with what other local schools are doing. Has anyone in charge stopped to ask if that is the goal in the first place?

School administrators need a vision for what excellence looks like in a school's music program. Look at the cathedral choirs of England, for instance. These programs did not start only for the sake of having concerts. They trained young singers to be musically literate. The program and performances were fruits of that activity. Boy choirs in Europe and the U.S. also provide some inspiration for training and performance opportunities. There are many YouTube videos of eventide singing from such groups. Or look to the choir colleges of the midwest like St. Olaf College in Minnesota where they have established a traditional repertoire of songs and styles our classical schools could gain from. A sure bet is the entire student body at New Saint Andrews College (in case you are tempted to think only music majors can sing) where the programming and concert selection are vast and sample some of the best of western music. Belmont University in Nashville also has some excellent work, if you stick to the hymns and liturgical song arrangements that they perform (my favorite is "Come, Thou Fount of Every Blessing"). Or look to some of the stronger classical Christian programs around the country. Many of their concerts can be found on YouTube. Christmas music from many of these groups mentioned often provides excellent vision in these areas. There is room for various forms and genres of music, if you choose wisely. Again, the arrangements are usually the difference. Look to the ACCS National Honor Choir for some excellent and challenging music choices.

Even established Christian college programs across the country will be influenced by modern tendencies when selecting music. Choose carefully. The choices and repertoire matter more than we think in our society today. Be bold enough to plunder the Egyptians where they are doing good work, but don't build a music program around the wrong kind of inspiration.

Vision is the beginning of a good music program. The head of school, not just the music department, needs to lead the whole school to a great vision for classical Christian education.

www.ingramcontent.com/pod-product-compliance
Lightning Source LLC
Chambersburg PA
CBHW071404290426
44108CB00014B/1679